The New York Yankees

Babe Ruth.

The New York Yankees

An Illustrated History

by Donald Honig

Crown Publishers, Inc. New York

Copyright © 1981 by Donald Honig

All rights reserved. No part of this book may be
reproduced or utilized in any form or by any means,
electronic or mechanical, including photocopying,
recording, or by any information storage and retrieval
system, without permission in writing from the
publisher.

Inquiries should be addressed to Crown Publishers, Inc.,
One Park Avenue, New York, New York 10016

Printed in the United States of America

Published simultaneously in Canada by General
Publishing Company Limited

Library of Congress Cataloging in Publication Data

Honig, Donald
The New York Yankees.

Includes index.
1. New York Yankees (Baseball Club)—History
I. Title.
GV 875.N4H66 1981 796.357′64′09471 81-3212
ISBN: 0-517-544962   AACR2

10 9 8 7 6 5 4 3 2 1

First Edition

Design: Robert Aulicino

For my daughter Catherine

By Donald Honig

Fiction

Sidewalk Caesar
Walk Like a Man
The Americans
Divide the Night
No Song to Sing
Judgment Night
The Love Thief
The Severith Style
Illusions
I Should Have Sold Petunias
The Last Great Season
Marching Home

Nonfiction

Baseball When the Grass Was Real
Baseball Between the Lines
The Man in the Dugout
The October Heroes
The Image of Their Greatness (with Lawrence Ritter)
The 100 Greatest Baseball Players of All Time (with Lawrence Ritter)
The Brooklyn Dodgers: An Illustrated Tribute
The New York Yankees: An Illustrated History

For Young Readers

Frontiers of Fortune
Jed McLane and Storm Cloud
Jed McLane and the Stranger
In the Days of the Cowboy
Up From the Minor Leagues
Dynamite
Johnny Lee
The Journal of One Davey Wyatt
An End of Innocence
Way to Go Teddy
Playing For Keeps
Breaking In
The Professional
Coming Back
Fury on Skates
Hurry Home
Running Harder
Going the Distance
Winter Always Comes

Editor

Blue and Gray: Great Writings of the Civil War
The Short Stories of Stephen Crane

Contents

Acknowledgments

I am deeply indebted to a number of people for their generous assistance in photo research and help in gathering the photographs reproduced in this book. Special thanks are due Jack Redding, librarian of the National Baseball Hall of Fame and Museum in Cooperstown, New York, for his interest and his help. Also, to Michael P. Aronstein, president of the Card Memorabilia Associates, Ltd., in Amawalk, New York, for the generosity of his assistance and the unique wisdom and enthusiasm he brings to his work. And to Lawrence Wahl and David Szen of the New York Yankees' publicity office, Neil Sakow of Simsbury, Connecticut, and Lawrence Ritter and David Markson of New York City. I would also like to thank those New York Yankee ballplayers who allowed the use of pictures from their personal albums. The remaining photographs are from the following sources: Louis Requena, Little Ferry, New Jersey: 275 (bottom right), 279 (bottom), 282 (top left), 288 (top left, bottom), 292 (bottom), 294 (bottom), 295 (bottom), 297 (top left), 299 (bottom); Ronald C. Modra, Port Washington, Wisconsin: 273, 275 (bottom left), 276, 277, 281 (top), 283 (bottom), 284 (right, bottom left), 285 (left), 286 (top right, bottom), 287 (bottom left and right), 290, 293, 296, 297 (bottom), 298 (bottom left), 299 (top); J. J. Donnelly, Pearl River, New York: 259, 274, 278 (top right, bottom), 279 (top right), 280, 282 (top right, bottom left), 283 (top), 284 (top left), 285 (top right), 286 (top left), 289, 291 (top left, top right), 292 (top left, top right), 294 (top left), 295 (top left, top right), 297 (top right), 298 (top right, bottom right), 301 (left, bottom right); New York Yankees: 225 (top left), 239 (bottom right), 298 (top left), 300 (top center, top right, bottom left).

Prologue

hey are a myth maker's dream and a storyteller's delight. Not only have they contributed names and feats to American folklore but they have had the good dramatic sense to perform their rituals in a majestic stadium located in the world's most conspicuous city.

Time in its passage works changes upon all things. Applying this lofty proposition to baseball, one is aware how the images of most teams have undergone changes with the years. There have been changes in their characteristics, their styles, their ball parks, their uniforms, for some even the cities in which they play.

One team, however, has resisted time's caprices and sustained an image for so long that the image has evolved into legend. Year by year, player by player, the New York Yankees have risen to a place of supremacy unmatched by any other team, not only in the record books but in the fans' imaginations. Strength, power, wealth, and success have been their hallmark as they continue as the big team in America's favorite pastime, a fabled name at work in a great stadium filled with the rousing ghosts of past glories.

But when examined more closely, the vast tapestry that is Yankee history becomes a portrait of myriad details; it is a tapestry woven strand by strand by mighty bats and flashing feet and strong arms. The magic is imbued with sweat and muscle.

This book is about the men who have created, inherited, conveyed, and endowed this magic. But one must not succumb too deeply to temptation: yes, it is magic, but only when one takes the long perspective and sees at a glance those full majestic careers of Babe Ruth and his numerous crown princes. The pictures within this book, however, bring us face to face with those young men of long ago, of yesterday, and of today, enabling us to see once more the shadows of unremembered summers, the soft suspension of infield dust, the stride and the effort of the men who, thread by thread, wove and continue to weave the tapestry of Yankee legend.

A rare action shot at Hilltop Park, around 1909. The Yankees are hosting the Chicago White Sox. Note the path between the mound and home plate. Note also how close Chase is playing in and what a lead he is giving the runner. It is conceivable the bases are loaded and Hal is looking for a play at the plate. In any event, from where the right fielder is playing it is obvious the batter is a dead pull hitter. All in all, a fine summer's afternoon in New York, long, long ago.

1

**A Slow
Beginning**

(1903-1919)

The New York Yankees joined the American League in 1903, when the league was beginning its third year. Its first two years had been stormy ones as it sought both to compete and coexist with the National League, in business since 1876. The older circuit greeted the establishment of the new league pretty much as one might expect—with contempt and hostility.

The American League was the creation of Byron Bancroft Johnson. Ban, as he was known, had been president of the highly successful Western League, a minor league in the Midwest. Ban changed the name of his operation to American and declared it a major league, expanding eastward to include franchises in Philadelphia, Boston, Washington, and Baltimore.

Johnson, however, knew that it would take more than a rechristening and personal anointing to upgrade his league's status; only ballplayers could achieve that. So Johnson and his club owners began raiding National League rosters. Among the players who succumbed to the beckoning checkbooks of the new league were such luminaries as Cy Young, Iron Man McGinnity, Nap Lajoie, Jimmy Collins, Clark Griffith, and John McGraw.

Johnson ran his league with an iron hand. This hand was lifted time and again against the hot-tempered player-manager of the Baltimore Orioles, John McGraw, a ferocious umpire baiter. (Johnson demanded that his umpires be treated with respect, a novel notion in those early days.) After having been suspended by Johnson for a large part of the 1902 season, the seething McGraw decided on a back-alley maneuver to avenge himself.

McGraw was the brains behind an arrangement whereby John T. Brush, chairman of the National League Executive Committee, bought the Orioles. This was having a fox in the hen house, and Johnson almost choked on his own fury when he heard about it. After taking over the franchise, Brush, in connivance with McGraw, pulled off a bit of highhanded sabotage by releasing a number of Baltimore's star players, including McGinnity, Roger Bresnahan, Joe Kelley, and McGraw himself, all of whom quickly signed with National League clubs. By the end of the 1902 season McGraw was managing the New York Giants; Brush bought the team the next year. Fielding a skeleton crew, Baltimore finished the season and then dropped out of the major leagues, not to return until 1954.

The evaporation of the Baltimore franchise gave Johnson an opening in his circuit and the oppor-

tunity to move into the city he felt would finally put the American League on equal footing with the National. When Brush heard the American League wanted to invade New York, he began using his Tammany Hall connections to prevent it. Whenever the new club announced it was going to purchase a plot of land upon which to build its park, the city quickly countered with an announcement that it planned to run a new street through it.

Johnson finally found a couple of politically muscular customers of his own who were interested in bankrolling the new ball club. They were Big Bill Devery and Frank Farrell, a pair of tough, hard-bitten, derby-hatted gentlemen who knew their way around the city's murkier corridors of influence even more persuasively than did Brush. Devery was a former chief of police (reputedly the most corrupt ever, quite a distinction in those palmy days), and Farrell was a well-known gambler and racehorse owner. Together they succeeded in bringing the American League to New York.

The new team was called the Highlanders, primarily because their ball park was built on a tract of land in Washington Heights, Manhattan Island's most elevated point. The name was never very popular with the fans (nor with linotype operators, who had trouble squeezing it into headlines), and gradually the more American-sounding "Yankees" became attached to the club. It is unclear when, how, and where the name originated.

An army of workmen hammered together a ball park for the new team on a tract of land on Broadway between 165th and 168th streets (currently the site of the Columbia Presbyterian Medical Center), barely getting it ready for the opening of the 1903 season. This modest little park, whose wooden grandstands could accommodate 15,000 people, was formally known as the New York American League Ball Park, but was commonly called Hilltop Park.

By 1903 the National League realized its rival had come to stay and reluctantly accepted the fact. By mutual consent the two leagues agreed to stop shaking their fists at one another and, more importantly, to stop pirating each other's players. Before this agreement went into effect, however, Johnson had managed to pluck a few more ripe ones from the National League vines, including Pittsburgh's ace right-hander Jack Chesbro, who joined the New York team.

Johnson induced Clark Griffith, then player-manager of the Chicago White Sox, to manage the Highlanders. Griffith, who was later to own the Washington Senators for many years, was a crafty right-handed pitcher who had earned the nickname "Old Fox." Though he did some pitching for his new club, the thirty-three-year-old Griffith's playing days were winding down.

The first New York American League team featured two outstanding players, Chesbro and Wee Willie Keeler. Willie—to whom is attributed the hitter's golden rule, "Hit 'em where they ain't"—gave the New Yorkers some fine years, though his finest were behind him. Chesbro won 21 games and helped bring the Highlanders home in fourth place, a respectable finish for a new club. Attendance for that first season was 211,808, which is about what the club's descendants will draw today for a four-game series against a contender.

Attendance more than doubled the next year as the Highlanders made a run for the pennant that ended on the last day of the season. Keeler led the hitters with a .343 average, but it was Chesbro who stole the show, putting on a season-long performance that was awesome. Happy Jack, as the big, good-natured spitballer was known, started 51 games, completed 48, worked 455 innings, and ended with a 41–12 record. His win and complete-game totals remain major-league records, unlikely ever to be broken.

Chesbro made thousands of pitches that year; unfortunately, he is remembered for one, virtually the last he made that season. The Highlanders battled Boston (then known as the Pilgrims) down to the last day. The Boston club, leading New York by one game, was at Hilltop Park for a double-header; the Highlanders needed a sweep in order to win the pennant. In the top of the ninth inning of the first game, with the score tied 2–2, Boston had a man on third and two out. Chesbro uncorked a wild pitch, allowing what turned out to be the winning run to score.

That was as close as the Highlanders were to come to a pennant until they actually won one as the Yankees in 1921, although in 1906 Griffith again brought his club in second, three games behind Chicago's Hitless Wonders (a well-earned designation: they batted .230 and hit all of six home runs that year).

Joining the Highlanders in 1905 was a twenty-two-year-old first baseman from California who would become the team's greatest player until the arrival of Babe Ruth in 1920. His name was Hal Chase and he was one of the most enigmatic men ever to play big-league ball. If we can rely on the word of those who saw him play, he was an utter magician around first base. He is credited with having possessed remarkable grace, speed, and agility. A left-handed thrower and right-handed batter (a rare combination), Chase was in many ways a pioneer at first base, playing away from the bag at a time when this was not commonly done, charging bunts, and throwing runners out at second or third, also a rare practice then. In an age when the bunt was a frequent offensive weapon, Chase's skills were of inestimable value to a club.

He was an engaging character, intelligent, witty, charming. He was also, apparently, unscrupulous and dishonest. Once described as having a "corkscrew brain," Chase was known to consort with gamblers and was suspected by many, including some of his own teammates and one of his managers, of throwing games. It has been alleged that Chase was the go-between for the gamblers and the Chicago White Sox players who conspired to throw the 1919 World Series. He remained with the New York club until 1913, when manager Frank Chance (of Tinker-to-Evers-to-Chance renown), fed up with Chase's dubious performances on the field, traded him. The odor of Prince Hal's reputation has remained strong enough to keep him out of the Hall of Fame.

In 1908 the team sank to last place. Season attendance was around 300,000, one-third of what McGraw's swaggering Giants were pulling in. New York was and remained for many years a National League town; more specifically, a Giant town. McGraw's clubs were crisply efficient winners and hence crowd pleasers. Outside of the flashy Chase, the Highlanders had no one who could attract paying customers.

Failure inevitably dooms a manager, and in mid-season 1908 Griffith was replaced by the team's shortstop, Arthur Norman Elberfeld, also known as the "Tabasco Kid," nicknames being what they were in those days. Elberfeld managed the team to a 27–71 record during his tenure. The Kid's winning percentage figured out to .276, five points better than his own lifetime batting average. When a skipper's batting average is about the same as his winning percentage he had better keep his bags packed. This proved to be true in Elberfeld's case.

The Yankees, as they were then coming to be known, began a revolving-door policy for their managers. In 1909–1910 the chief was George Stallings, in 1911 Hal Chase, in 1912 Harry Wolverton, in 1913–1914 Frank Chance. Despite all this fresh brain power, the team finished in the second division five out of those six years. There was little for fans to cheer about during these years of gloom, and in fact few fans were coming up to Hilltop Park to do that little cheering. Every club in the league with the exception of the Washington Senators was outdrawing the Yankees.

Losing became a way of life at Hilltop Park. Roger Peckinpaugh, a bright young shortstop the Yankees acquired from Cleveland in 1913, had this to say years later about the team: "The Yankees were at that time what we used to call a joy club. Lots of joy and lots of losing. Nobody thought we could win and most of the time we didn't. But it didn't seem to bother the boys too much. They would start singing songs in the infield right in the middle of the game." Their chief concern was not to get beaten too badly. The 1913 squad was particularly harmless, hitting only nine home runs all year. (The 1939 Yankees once hit eight homers in a single game, but the world was different then.)

The Yankees abandoned Hilltop Park after the 1912 season and moved into the Polo Grounds as tenants of the Giants. This change of scenery did not improve the club's fortunes either artistically or financially. Devery and Farrell, who had bought the team ten years before with such high hopes for success, were becoming disenchanted. Constant quarreling had chilled their personal relationship, and more important, they were losing money. They began looking around for a buyer for the barely breathing franchise.

For a few years a couple of red-hot Giant fans had been trying to buy that team, but the Giants were not for sale. Hearing that the Yankees were on the market, McGraw suggested to these gentlemen that they buy the club. Negotiations were begun late in 1914, and in January 1915 the deal was consummated. The price was $460,000 (a year's salary for a .280 hitter today). The deal was the turning point in Yankee history, and consequently for baseball history as well.

One of the new owners went by the magnificent handle of Captain Tillinghast L'Hommedieu Huston. He was an amiable, oversized Ohioan who had made his pile in construction in Cuba after the Spanish-American War. Before that he had been an engineering officer in the United States Army. The other new owner, a man who was to make an indelible mark on baseball by launching the Yankee dynasty, was a wealthy New York socialite and former congressman named Colonel Jacob Ruppert. Jake's title was an honorary one, conferred by New York's Governor David Bennett Hill in 1889, when Ruppert was twenty-two. His fortune originated in his family's brewery, one of the city's most prosperous.

Outside of their interest in baseball, the new owners had little in common. Huston was big, untidy, and gregarious, enjoying the company of ballplayers and sports writers. Ruppert, a lifelong bachelor, was compact, an impeccable dresser, cordial but aloof. The stronger personality of the two, he was installed as the team's president, Huston as vice-president. Inside of the quiet Ruppert burned a fervent desire to win, a not uncommon quality in the sports world; but Jake was willing to back it up with greenbacks. He was a big spender but a shrewd one, aware of his fellow New Yorkers' eagerness to back a winner. (The high-riding Giants, who outdrew everyone in the National League, were his example.)

The new owners hired a fresh manager, Wild Bill Donovan, a thirty-nine-year-old former right-handed pitcher who had just wound up a long career with the Detroit Tigers. Wild Bill ran the club for three years, his best showing a fourth-place finish in 1916. After a sixth-place finish in 1917 Donovan got the boot, and the Yankees went shopping for their eighth manager in sixteen years.

On the surface things continued to look dismal. But some sunlight was starting to filter through the clouds. In 1915 the Yankees bought righty Bob Shawkey from the Philadelphia Athletics. In a few years Shawkey blossomed into the team's best pitcher since Chesbro. A year later the New Yorkers purchased one of Connie Mack's stalwarts, Frank ("Home Run") Baker, an outstanding third baseman. At first base was youngster Wally Pipp, who a decade later became one of baseball's imperishable footnotes. But meanwhile the left-handed swinger inaugurated what was to become a Yankee tradition—leading the league in home runs. Wally achieved this two years running, 1916 and 1917, with totals of 12 and 9.

Ruppert and Huston disagreed as to who should be their next manager. Huston wanted one of his cronies, Wilbert Robinson, then managing the Brooklyn Dodgers. Ruppert said no.

While the partners were trying to agree on a new skipper, Huston went off to France with the army, America having entered World War I in April of 1917. Acting on his own, Ruppert hired the manager of the St. Louis Cardinals, Miller Huggins. When Huston received word of this in France, he sent Ruppert a series of blistering letters and cables accusing Jake of contempt, betrayal, double-cross, and whatever else he could think of, right on up to high treason. Ruppert, to the manner born, was unperturbed by his partner's fulminations. Jake, who had hired Huggins at the urging of Ban Johnson, was convinced he had made a good choice. And as a matter of fact, he had. The breach between Ruppert and Huston was never fully mended.

Miller Huggins, who managed the Yankees from 1918 to the end of the 1929 season, was thirty-nine years old when he took over the club, and had a rather undistinguished career as a National League second baseman and manager behind him. Huggins, who at 5'4" looked like the team mascot when standing with some of his massive sluggers, was a man of considerable intelligence, having studied law before deciding to make baseball his career. He exuded a sense of strength, dignity, and integrity that rendered his slightness of frame irrelevant. Everyone who played for him, including that great

unmanageable himself, Babe Ruth, came to admire and respect him.

Not even Huggins, however, could produce miracles. In 1918, his first year, he brought his team in fourth. In 1919 a spirited Yankee team finished third and set a new attendance record by drawing 619,000 customers. The team's 45 home runs led the league, and Shawkey was a 20-game winner.

As the nation headed into the zaniest, most freewheeling decade in its history, one of its baseball teams was about to emerge from the shadows and become a powerhouse that captured the imaginations of Americans everywhere. The Yankees were about to soar behind the lethal bat and infectious personality of one who would soon become, along with George Washington and Abraham Lincoln, the most recognized American name in the world.

Hilltop Park soon after its construction in 1903.

Frank Farrell, the man responsible for bringing the American League to New York, in the early years of the century.

Clark Griffith, first manager of the New York American League baseball team. He later became manager and long-time owner of the Washington Senators.

Jimmy Williams was the Highlanders' regular second baseman from the beginning of their history to 1907. Jimmy's best year was 1906, when he batted .277.

Wid Conroy played the infield and outfield for the Highlanders from 1903 through 1908. His best year was 1905, when he batted .273.

Wee Willie Keeler demonstrating the art of bunting. Keeler joined the Highlanders in 1903 after 11 years in the National League. Willie played for the Highlanders until 1909, hitting .343 for them in 1904.

Kid Elberfeld, Highlander shortstop from 1903 through 1909 and its manager in 1908. The Kid batted .306 in 1906, his best showing.

John Dwight Chesbro, better known as Jack, and still better known as the man who won 41 games for the Highlanders in 1904. Jack's next best year in New York was 1906, when he was 24–16. He pitched for the Highlanders from 1903 to 1909.

John Peter ("Red") Kleinow, catcher for the Highlanders from 1904 to 1910. Red must have been a good glove man, since his lifetime average was .213 (though he did get up to .264 in 1907). ➔

Al Orth pitched for the New Yorkers from 1904 to 1908. He outdid himself with a 27–17 season in 1906. The year before he was 18–18, a year later 14–21.

Jack Chesbro in 1906.

Right-hander Bill Hogg pitched for the Highlanders from 1905 to 1908. He was 14–13 in 1906, his best year. Bill retired at the end of the 1908 season and a year later died at the age of twenty-nine.

Hal Chase.

Outfielder Charlie Hemphill was an American League veteran when he joined the Yankees in 1908. He remained until 1911. He batted .297 in 1908, his top year in New York.

Highlander utility man George Moriarity. George was with the club from 1906 to 1908, batting .277 in '07. He was traded to Detroit in 1909, a team he later managed.

Tom Hughes pitched for the Yankees from 1906 to 1910 with middling success. Later he became a 20-game winner for the Boston Braves.

Right-hander Walter ("Rube") Manning pitched for the Yankees from 1907 to 1910. Rube's most productive year was 1908, when he was 13–16 for the last-place New Yorkers.

Jack Powell joined the Highlanders in 1904, was 23–19, and was traded the following year.

One of the earliest spring-training pictures ever taken shows the Yankees on the porch of their hotel in Hot Springs, Arkansas, in 1908. Front row, left to right: unidentified, Lou Kleinow, Bill Dahlen, Kid Elberfeld, Bill Hogg, unidentified, Jack Chesbro. Standing above Chesbro is Wee Willie Keeler, next to Keeler is manager Clark Griffith, and the young gentleman next to Griffith is none other than Branch Rickey. Rickey had been a utility man the year before, batting .182. He did not make the team in 1908. Next to Rickey is Sam Crane, a well-known sports writer of the day. The elderly man next to Crane is not identified, but the man next to him is Jake Stahl, who played some first base for the team that year. The other men are not identified.

Here are the Yankees again in Hot Springs in 1908, doing their best to get around town. Left to right: unidentified, Chesbro, Kleinow, Elberfeld, unidentified, Stahl, Orth, Hogg, Keeler, Griffith, Sam Crane.

George Stallings, Yankee manager in 1909 and 1910.

William ("Birdie") Cree gave the Yankees some fine years during his 1908–1915 tenure in their outfield. His .348 batting average in 1911 was the club's highest until Ruth's .376 in 1920.

Harry Wolter, Yankee outfielder from 1910 to 1913. Harry's best year was 1911, when he batted .304.

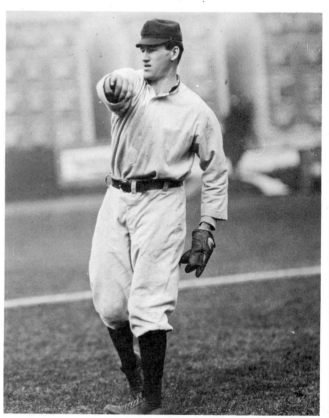

Jimmy Austin, the Yankees' regular third baseman from 1909 to 1910. Jimmy batted .231 and .218 and was traded to the St. Louis Browns, where he played for the next dozen years.

Ed Sweeney, Yankees catcher from 1908 to 1915. His best season with the bat was 1912, when he hit .268.

While the Yankees were struggling, the big team in New York was John McGraw's Giants. John J. and four of his stalwarts in 1912; left to right: Fred Merkle, Larry Doyle, Christy Mathewson, McGraw, Fred Snodgrass. Three different uniforms, but Giants all.

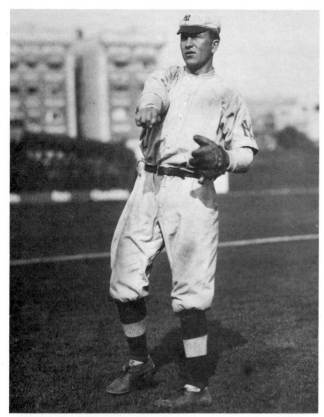

Bert Daniels played in the Yankees outfield from 1910 to 1913. He batted .286 in 1911.

You're looking at a man who got away—left-hander Jim ("Hippo") Vaughan was 12–11 with the Yankees in 1910, with a 1.82 ERA and five shutouts. The following year he slumped to 8–11. He got off poorly in 1912 and the Yankees waived him to Washington. Washington sent him to the minors, the Cubs picked him up, and Big Jim went on to become one of the great pitchers of the World War I era.

Roy Hartzell played infield and outfield with the Yankees from 1911 to 1916. His best season was 1911, when he batted .296 after being obtained from the Browns.

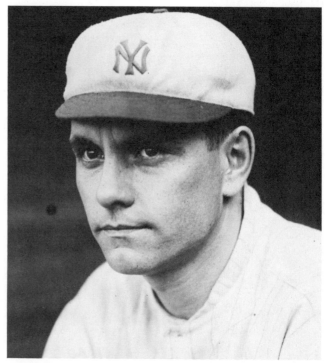

Canadian-born Russ Ford astounded the Yankees and the rest of the league in his rookie year with a 26–6 record and 1.65 earned-run average. The following year, 1911, he was 21–11. His descent was as startling and as abrupt as his rise. He had two losing seasons and by 1914 he was gone.

Right-hander Jack Warhop spent his entire eight-year big-league career (1908–1915) with the Yankees. His top years were 1910 and 1911, when he was 14–14 and 13–13.

Right-hander Ray Fisher worked for the Yankees from 1910 to 1917, with a peak season of 18–11 in 1915.

Righty Urban Shocker pitched for the Yankees in 1916 and 1917 and fared nicely. The New Yorkers then made a mistake and traded him to the Browns, where he became one of the best, a four-time 20-game winner. The Yankees got him back in 1925.

Harry Wolverton managed the Yankees in 1912, finished last and was gone.

Roger Peckinpaugh, first of the great Yankee shortstops, was obtained from Cleveland in 1913. He remained with New York until 1921. His best year with the bat was .306 in 1919. When Chance resigned in September 1914, Roger, at the age of twenty-three, ran the team for the last few weeks of the season. He remains the youngest man ever to manage a big-league team.

Ray Caldwell pitched for the Yankees from 1910 to 1918 and had some fine years; the best were 1914 and 1915, when he was 18–9 and 19–16.

Ray Caldwell getting some attention from the trainer at the Yankees' spring training camp in Macon, Georgia.

It is April 1913 and there is an on-the-field discussion in progress. Washington manager Clark Griffith is trying to point out the facts to the home-plate umpire while Yankee skipper Frank Chance (in dark sweater) stands by. The man standing just above the home-plate umpire is Walter Johnson.

Fritz Maisel, shown here in 1915, was with the Yankees from 1913 to 1917, mostly at third base. His best year was 1915, when he batted .281. In 1914 Fritz led the league with 74 stolen bases, still the Yankees all-time high.

Frank Chance, one of the great heroes of Chicago baseball, managed the Yankees in 1913 and 1914 with little success.

Catcher Les Nunamaker played for the Yankees from 1914 to 1917, batting .296 in 1916.

April 2, 1914: the Brooklyn Dodgers are opening their brand new ball park, Ebbets Field, with an exhibition game with the Yankees. Brooklyn manager Wilbert Robinson sand Yankee skipper Frank Chance are making it official with a handshake.

Fritz Maisel bunting away in a preseason exhibition game between the Yankees and the Boston Braves. The catcher is Bill Rariden, the umpire Bill Dineen. The year is 1913.

New owner Jacob Ruppert (right) poses with his manager, Bill Donovan, and Al Smith, then a New York City sheriff and a future governor of New York and Democratic presidential candidate. Note the souvenir in Al's right hand.

Wild Bill Donovan, Yankee manager from 1915 to 1917.

Tillinghast L'Hommedieu ("Cap") Huston in 1916.

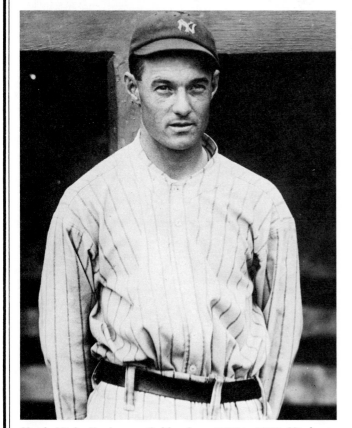

Hugh High, Yankee outfielder from 1915 to 1918. His best year was 1916, when he batted .263.

His real name was Francesco Stephano Pezzolo, but Yankee fans knew him as Ping Bodie when he played in their outfield from 1918 to 1921. Ping's top year was 1920, when he batted .295.

Bob Shawkey. Obtained from the Philadelphia Athletics in 1915, Bob became a four-time 20-game winner for the Yankees, for whom he pitched from 1915 to 1927.

Dazzy Vance had brief trials with the Yankees in 1915 and 1918 and didn't impress anyone. In 1922, however, he came up with the Brooklyn Dodgers and became one of the great pitchers of all time.

Slugger, third baseman, and proud father—Frank ("Home Run") Baker with daughters Ottlie, left, and Janice.

Miller Huggins when he was playing second base for the St. Louis Cardinals, around 1910. From the way he's choking up on that bat you know Huggins didn't go up there swinging for home runs.

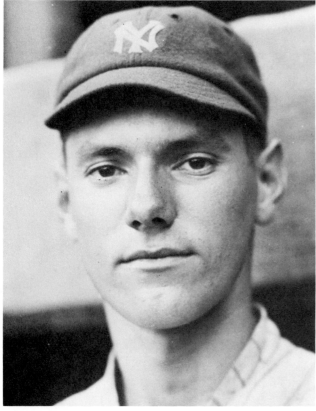

Left-hander Herbert ("Hank") Thormahlen pitched for the Yankees from 1917 to 1920. His best showing was in 1919, when he was 13–10.

Miller Huggins.

Obtained from the Browns in exchange for Urban Shocker, Del Pratt gave the Yankees three solid years at second base (1918–1920), with batting averages of .275, .292, and .314, before being dealt to the Red Sox as part of the Wait Hoyt deal.

Herold ("Muddy") Ruel was a part-time catcher for the Yankees from 1917 to 1920. After batting .268 in 1920, he was sent to the Red Sox as part of the package for Waite Hoyt. The Red Sox, with no sense at all in those days, soon traded him to Washington, where he became a workhorse behind the plate, a .300 hitter, and enjoyed a long career in the American League.

Roger Peckinpaugh in 1920.

George Mogridge, a good left-hander who pitched for the Yankees from 1915 to 1920. He was 17–13 in 1918, his best year. He was traded to Washington in 1921 and gave the Senators some fine seasons.

Jack Quinn was with the Yankees twice, from 1909 to 1912 and from 1919 to 1921. The right-hander's best years were 18–12 in 1910 and 18–10 in 1920. Quinn pitched in the big leagues until 1933, when he was forty-nine years old.

This young man had his priorities all wrong when he tried out for the Yankees as a left-handed pitcher in 1919, 1920, and 1921. His name is Frank ("Lefty") O'Doul, and after giving up pitching he returned to the big leagues as a National League outfielder and compiled a .349 lifetime average over a seven-year career. The Yankees were on the right track with the youngster, since during his brief stints with the club they used him more often as a pinch hitter than as a pitcher.

Duffy Lewis was just about over the hill when the Yankees obtained the fine veteran from the Red Sox in 1919. Duffy played in New York for two years, batting .272 and .271, and then faded from the scene.

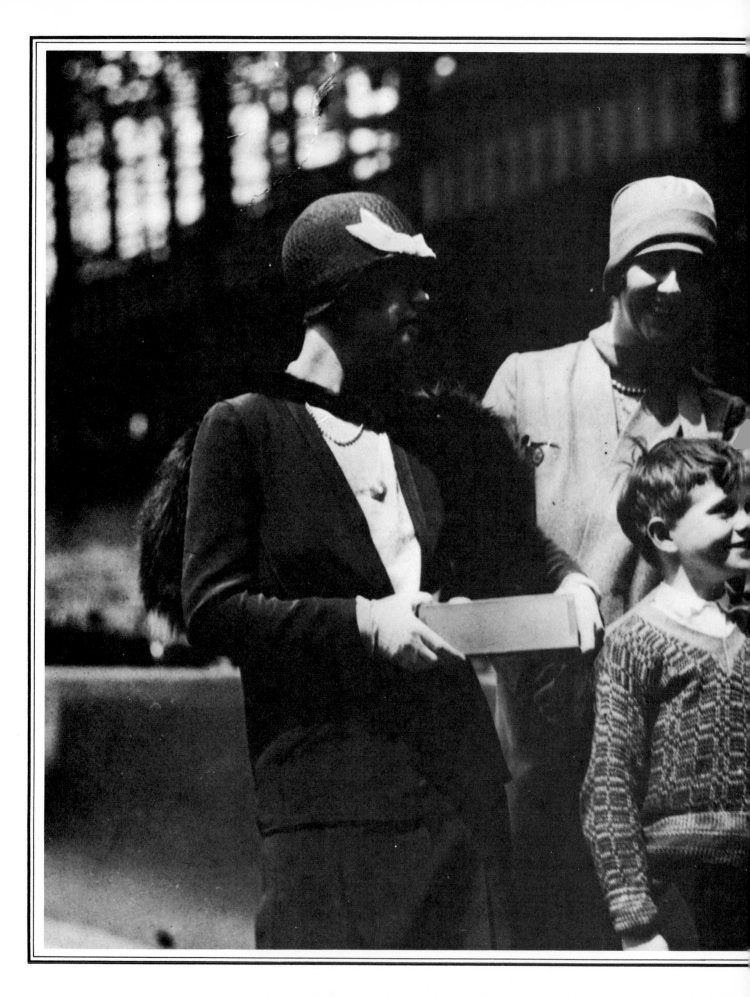

2
Mr. Ruth
Comes to Town
(1920-1929)

In 1916, Boston Red Sox left-hander George Herman ("Babe") Ruth won 23 games and led the American League with a 1.75 earned-run average. The following year he won 24 games and posted an ERA of 2.01; he also batted .325. In 1918 his potent bat made him a part-time outfielder, reducing his role on the mound. He was 13–7 pitching that year and .300 at home plate, tying for the league lead in home runs with 11 (the league record at the time was 16). In 1919 he spent most of his time in the outfield and responded by leading the league in runs batted in and by hitting an astounding, record-shattering 29 home runs. The twenty-four-year-old Boston phenomenon had suddenly replaced Ty Cobb as the game's most exciting player. The big rollicking Paul Bunyan of an athlete was the toast of Boston, and Red Sox fans were set for a continuation of the glory that had brought pennants and world championships to Boston in 1912, 1915, 1916, and 1918.

But there was a problem in Boston by the name of Harry Frazee. Harry owned the team. He probably liked baseball, but he liked producing Broadway shows even more. Unfortunately for Harry, and even more unfortunately for Red Sox fans, many of these shows were turkeys, and Frazee was constantly in need of cash. (Unwittingly, New York's drama critics were bringing Babe Ruth closer to New York each time they thumbed their noses at one of Harry's efforts.) Jake Ruppert had the cash and Frazee had the ballplayers. A beautiful partnership was in the making.

On December 26, 1919, New Yorkers were handed a post-Christmas present named Babe Ruth. In the most stunning player transaction in the game's history, the Yankees obtained Ruth for around $125,000. It was a lot of money in those days, but it was a spit in the ocean when one realizes that owning Babe Ruth was as good as having a license to print money.

He was one of a kind and there can never be another one. The man was a combination of ballplaying talent, personality, magnetism, show business, drama, and innocence that had to have been handcrafted by some celestial artisan who is probably too pleased to want to top himself and too wise to try.

This big, homely, moon-faced kid, so filled with power and physical poetry, was the son of a Baltimore saloon keeper who, unable to handle him, turned him over to an industrial school managed by a Catholic order. Sports were emphasized, and young George excelled. It has been said that baseball probably saved the unruly kid from a life of unsavory pursuits. If this is true, then Ruth soon repaid his debt with interest to spare.

If Babe Ruth had not appeared when he did it might have been necessary for baseball to invent him. Reeling from the disclosures of the fixed 1919 World Series, the game was in danger of losing the public's faith and trust. But before too much cynicism could seriously affect baseball, Ruth came roaring upon the scene with feats of heroism that were utterly without precedent.

Not only did he help save the sport, not only was he the myth upon which the Yankee dynasty was created, but he also changed the way the game was played. By hitting a recently juiced-up ball for prodigious distances, he helped end the era, personified by Cobb, of bunt and slap and steal.

Boston may have been stunned and outraged by the deal, but truth be told, New York was the only place for this colossus to play. After closing the deal with the Red Sox, the Yankees signed Ruth to a two-year contract at $20,000 per year. That may be three days' income for certain of today's worthies, but back then it was probably five times the average salary. Whatever they paid him, he was a bargain. In 1920, Ruth's first year in pinstripes, Yankee attendance more than doubled, climbing to almost 1.3 million. They came to see the Babe, and the show he put on in 1920 was awesome. Fans wondered if he could top his record of 29 home runs; he hit 54, and along the way drove in 137 runs, scored 158, and batted .376.

In spite of Ruth's rewriting of the record book, the best the Yankees could manage was a third-place finish, just three thin games behind. Submarine-throwing right-hander Carl Mays, obtained from the Red Sox the year before, won 26 games and Shawkey again won 20, but behind them the pitching faltered.

Ruppert, smelling a pennant, knew where to go for help (Jake no doubt cheered every time another Frazee show went down the Broadway drain). After having sold Ruth, Frazee probably figured he could get away with anything—which he did. Over the next few years an array of players came down from Boston to New York that included, besides Ruth and Mays, pitchers Waite Hoyt, Herb Pennock, Bullet Joe Bush, and Sad Sam Jones; catcher Wally Schang; shortstop Everett Scott; and third baseman Joe Dugan. By 1923 the rape of the Red Sox had been completed. A good year in Boston was virtual assurance of a career in New York. Beginning in 1922, the Red Sox spent eight of the next nine years in last place while the Yankees took six pennants in eight years. ("Yankee dynasty my ear," muttered an old-time Red Socker. "That was a Boston dynasty in Yankee uniforms.")

The 1921 Yankees won the club's first pennant, finishing with 98 victories, 4½ games ahead of Cleveland. Ruth was even better that year than he had been in 1920. For the third straight year (including his last year in Boston) he set a home-run record, hitting 59, drove in 170 runs and scored 177 (both new records) and batted .378. He now had a slugging partner, outfielder Bob Meusel, possessor of one of the game's great throwing arms. Meusel, whom the Yankees had purchased from the Pacific Coast League, hit 24 home runs, tying him for second place, and drove in 135 runs. The ex-Red Sox pitchers Mays and Hoyt won 46 games between them, Mays's 27 leading the league.

The Yankees led the league with 134 home runs, an achievement already familiar to them and one that would become even more so in the future. Between 1915 and 1947, a span of 33 seasons, they led in home runs 28 times.

With the Giants taking what would be the first of four straight pennants, the 1921 World Series was played entirely at the Polo Grounds. McGraw, disgruntled by his tenants' success and resentful of Ruth's conquest of what had always been a Giant town, had his team primed.

For several years baseball had experimented with a best-of-nine World Series, and 1921 was the last time this number was employed. McGraw's team took the series in eight, five games to three, despite the fact that both Mays and Hoyt opened with 3–0 shutouts. McGraw's pitchers held the Yankees to a collective .207 batting average. Ruth, hampered by a bad arm, played only six games and hit just one homer.

After the series, Ruth and Meusel went on a barnstorming tour around the country in direct contravention of a rule that forbade postseason playing by World Series participants. The rule's purpose was to insure that none of the series luster was compromised after the championship had been decided. Ruth, who had earned large sums of money barnstorming after the two previous seasons, was aware of the rule but decided to ignore it. One can hardly blame him; by 1921 he was already well on his way to being proclaimed a living deity. He was the biggest name in sports. It seemed natural to assume that the rules that applied to mere mortals did not apply to him. But he was wrong, for he suddenly found himself in the ring with a severe,

uncompromising gentleman named Kenesaw Mountain Landis. Landis, a federal judge, had been hired by the club owners after the scandal of the 1919 World Series and given the title of commissioner of baseball, with dictatorial powers to oversee the wayward game. The first serious challenge to Landis's authority came, almost inevitably, from Ruth.

The judge told Ruth and Meusel not to go on the tour. They went anyway. Landis bided his time and then let fire: the two Yankee sluggers were fined the amount of their serie's shares, around $3,500, and suspended for the first six weeks of the 1922 season. The ruling outraged the Babe and hurt the Yankees badly. But it established one thing beyond all doubt—tough and unforgiving authority had come to baseball.

Though deprived of their two top crash men for the first thirty-odd games of the 1922 season, the Yankees managed to hold on to first place until the boys returned, and then settled down to a breathtaking pennant race with the St. Louis Browns. Led by George Sisler's .420 batting average and an array of .300 hitters, the Browns stayed in it until the end, losing to the Yankees by a heartbreaking one-game margin.

Playing 110 games, the Babe hit 35 home runs. Meusel batted .319, Wally Pipp .329, Wally Schang .319. Joe Bush had a superb 26–7 season and the consistent Bob Shawkey won 20 for the fourth time. Huggins ran a five-man rotation of Bush, Shawkey, Mays, Hoyt, and Jones through the league over and over again, the five righties starting 151 of the club's 154 games. When they weren't starting they were coming in from the bullpen. Overall, they accounted for 90 of the team's 94 wins.

McGraw's boys, however, made short work of the Yankees in the '22 series, taking four straight (one game was called because of darkness). Backed by timely hitting, the Giant pitchers put on quite a show, holding the Yanks to a batting average of .203. Ruth went 2 for 17 for a wretched .118 mark. The Yankees were a coming team, but John McGraw's Giants were still the lords of baseball.

Despite two straight World Series victories over his intracity rivals, McGraw was becoming increasingly irritated by the Yankees' success. The tenants were outdrawing the landlords by large margins and the Giants finally told the Yankees to pick up their bats and balls and go elsewhere.

The idea suited Ruppert just fine; the aristocratic colonel had never felt comfortable as a tenant. McGraw hoped the Yankees would move far away—

to Queens, for instance. Ruppert, however, hardly budged. He bought the land of what had been a lumberyard just across the Harlem River from the Polo Grounds. There, upon a nondescript chunk of Bronx real estate, Jake resolved to raise baseball's greatest showcase. And that is just what he did.

Construction began early in May 1922 and was finished twelve months later, just in time for the opening of the 1923 season. The cost was around $2 million. If Yankee Stadium remains a majestic sight even today, in an era of monumental baseball arenas, one can imagine the impact it made in 1923. It was the first three-tiered ball park ever built. In 1928 the triple-deck stands were extended beyond the foul pole in left field, and a similar expansion beyond the right-field foul pole was made in 1937. Lights were installed in 1946. The massive steel-and-concrete structure was immediately dubbed "The House That Ruth Built." The short right field (295 feet down the line) was tailored to Ruth's left-handed swing, and forever after the Yankees would be on the lookout for left-handed power hitters.

The Stadium opened on April 18, 1923. Bob Shawkey beat the Red Sox 4–1. Ruth, whose dramatic timing was as precise as ever, won the game with a three-run homer, thrilling a crowd estimated at more than 65,000.

Around this time Ruppert bought out Cap Huston and became sole owner of the Yankees. Relations between the two men had been chilly for years. Huston had never forgiven Jake for hiring Huggins, and probably forgave him even less for having been right. Ruppert paid Huston $1.5 million, about six times what Cap had laid out for his share eight years earlier.

Ruppert had a general manager running the team for him, one Edward Grant Barrow, who became a fixture in the Yankee front office for the next twenty-five years. A forceful personality and tight with a buck, Barrow had been managing the Red Sox when induced to come to New York (nobody in Boston, it seems, was safe). Besides presiding over the growth of the Yankee dynasty, Barrow's primary claim to fame is that he was the man who, while managing the Red Sox, switched Babe Ruth from the mound to the outfield.

The year 1923 was a glorious one for the Yankees. It actually began in January, when the New Yorkers completed the rape of the Red Sox by obtaining lefty Herb Pennock, a smooth curve baller who became one of the game's greatest southpaws. To get Pennock, the Yankees sent to New England nonentities named McMillan, Skinner, and Murray. It was typical of the deals the Yankees were making with the Red Sox in those days. Why Commissioner Landis never stepped in and put a stop to this systematic destruction of a ball club remains a mystery.

Sam Jones was 21–8, Pennock 19–6, the Babe hit 41 crowd pleasers and batted .393 (his best ever), and the Yankees breezed to their third straight pennant by 16 games. And again in the October sunshine they found John McGraw and his Giants waiting for them. But this time, alternating between the Polo Grounds and Yankee Stadium, the Yankees overthrew John J. in six games and won their first world championship. Second baseman Aaron Ward led the way with a .417 average and Ruth had his first great series, hitting three home runs and batting .368.

The Giants' hitting hero was a craggy-faced, bowlegged thirty-three-year-old journeyman outfielder. His inside-the-park home run won the first game for the Giants, and in the third game his shot into the right-field bleachers gave the Giants their other win by a 1–0 margin. Yankee fans would hear of him again in later years; his name was Casey Stengel.

Coming to bat 26 times for the Yankees that season was a muscular, left-handed-hitting, twenty-year-old first baseman named Henry Louis Gehrig, a New York City product born a few miles down the road in 1903, when the Yankees themselves were but two months old. In his 26 at bats Lou collected 11 hits, good for nine runs batted in and a .423 batting average. But Wally Pipp was still anchored at first and young Lou was sent to Hartford in the Eastern League for another year.

The Giants won an unprecedented fourth straight flag in 1924 and the Yankees almost matched them—almost. They finished two games behind the Washington Senators, who won their first pennant ever. Satisfaction for Yankee fans came with Ruth's league-leading 46 home runs and .378 batting average, and the fact that Washington beat the Giants in the World Series. Young Mr. Gehrig showed up again at the end of the year and hit .500 in his ten games. Hartford had seen the last of him.

The Yankees went to spring training in 1925 with the not unreasonable expectation of recapturing the pennant. But just before the season began, something went wrong. It was called "The Bellyache Heard 'Round the World," and it belonged, naturally, to the Babe. Ruth was a gargantuan character off the field as well as on. Not only was he the world's leading slugger, but he was also right up there as an eater, drinker, womanizer, and night crawler. The gods finally became either angry or jealous, and early in April Ruth keeled over with excruciating stomach pains.

Babe's trouble was diagnosed as an intestinal abscess, or ulcer. He was sent to New York for an operation, which kept him out of action until June. When he did return to action, his problems continued. His not playing up to par (he hit a very un-Ruthian .290 that year), all-night carousals ("I room with Babe Ruth's suitcase," said roommate Ping Bodie, giving birth to one of baseball's deathless lines), late arrivals at the ball park, and general disregard of all training rules finally exhausted his manager's patience. The explosion came late in the season, in St. Louis. Huggins suspended his star and put a sting into it with a $5,000 fine, a barrel of money even for Ruth, who was then making around $50,000 a year.

An outraged Ruth headed for New York, hoping to find sympathy from Ruppert and Barrow. He found, instead, two stony faces; the owner and the GM were in complete accord with their manager's actions. Humbled and contrite, Ruth apologized to Huggins and was reinstated in September. The Yankees, meanwhile, had dropped through the league like lead, finishing seventh.

As the dismal, disappointing season dragged to its conclusion, Huggins and Barrow were looking ahead with high expectations, and with good reason. One reason was in center field, where a minor-league acquisition named Earle Combs was patrolling in style and hitting with authority (.342 in his first full year). Combs had been purchased from Louisville, managed at that time by Joe McCarthy. McCarthy had suggested to the club's owner that they not make the deal unless the Yankees tossed in "the kid named Gehrig" they had at Hartford. The Yankees refused. "A few years later," McCarthy recalled with satisfaction in an interview late in life, "I wound up with both of them."

At shortstop, the veteran Scott was beginning to slip, but the Yankees already had a replacement in young Mark Koenig. Huggins benched Scott in early May, bringing to a halt the shortstop's remarkable consecutive-game streak at 1,307. It was then the record, and an impressive one. But on June 2, 1925, Wally Pipp got his famous headache and asked Huggins for the day off. If he had known what was going to happen, Pipp might have taken several aspirin and played. Huggins inserted young Gehrig at first base, and there Lou remained for 14 years—the Yankees' Rock of Gibraltar.

The handsome, powerful, self-effacing Gehrig was the closest thing to Ruth baseball would see for a long time, and there he was, batting behind the Babe in the same lineup. But a ferocious left-handed swing was about all they had in common. If you wanted to draw Ruth's personal opposite, you would have come up with a portrait of Gehrig. Lou stayed in shape, did not carouse, was quiet, shy, sensitive. He was a model for what the Yankees wanted their players to be—a gentleman who could bust a baseball out of sight.

The youngster had been attending Columbia University on a scholarship when Yankee scout Paul Krichell induced him to sign a Yankee contract. McGraw had actually signed him for the Giants several years earlier, sending him off to Hartford, where he played under the name Lewis, so as not to compromise his amateur status—Lou wanted to return to Columbia in the fall and play football. But the university found out about the contract and had it abrogated. Barring that, Lou would have ended up as "The Pride of the Giants." Gehrig hit .295 in his maiden year—the lowest he would ever hit—and popped 20 home runs.

There was a superb blend of youth and experience on the 1926 Yankees. Gehrig was 23; rookie second baseman Tony Lazzeri, purchased from the Pacific Coast League, was 22; shortstop Koenig was 23. Veteran Joe Dugan was at third. Ruth, Combs, and Meusel formed an incomparable outfield. Pat Collins was the regular catcher. The pitching staff, headed by Pennock, Hoyt, and Jones, had been augmented by the acquisition of right-handed spitballer Urban Shocker from the Browns (a reacquisition, actually, for the Yankees had had him originally and traded him to the Browns in 1918, one of their few trading mistakes; Urban became a four-time 20-game winner for St. Louis).

In an unprecedented upward surge, the Yankees went from their seventh-place finish in 1925 to win their fourth pennant in 1926, finishing three up on Cleveland. Gehrig batted .313, rookie Lazzeri hit .275 but drove in 114 runs, and Mr. Ruth, his bellyache and his bellyaching both in the past, batted .372 with 47 long ones and 155 runs batted in. Pennock won 23, Shocker 19, Hoyt 16.

The Yankees were expected to waltz through the series against the St. Louis Cardinals, who were in the big show for the first time. But player-manager Rogers Hornsby's team gave them a spirited seven-game battle and emerged the winners, in spite of Ruth's four home runs and some smart pitching by Pennock.

The 1926 series will always be remembered for Grover Cleveland Alexander's dramatic strikeout of Tony Lazzeri in the seventh inning of the seventh game. The thirty-nine-year-old Alex, traded from the Cubs to the Cardinals early in the season, had turned in complete-game victories in the second and sixth games. Hauled out of the bullpen by Hornsby to relieve starter Jess Haines (who had opened a blister on his pitching hand), the once-mighty Alexander found Lazzeri waiting for him with two out, the bases loaded, and the Cardinals winning 3–2. It was one of baseball's most dramatic moments, and the veteran hurler, calling on the craft and guile of a lifetime, fanned the young slugger on a series of back-breaking curve balls.

Alex stayed in to mow them down in the eighth and got the first two men in the ninth. Then, pitching carefully to "the big son of a bitch," as he matter-of-factly referred to Ruth, he walked him. Whereupon Babe, in what has been described as the only mistake he ever made on a ball field, tried to steal second. He was shot down by catcher Bob O'Farrell, Hornsby making the tag.

The 1927 Yankees, generally regarded as baseball's greatest team, fielded the same eight regulars as the '26 club. The difference between the two teams was the maturing of the younger players. Gehrig suddenly erupted into a force nearly as devastating as Ruth, batting .373, hitting 47 home runs, driving home 175 runs. Lazzeri jumped his average to .309 and again cleared the 100 mark in RBIs. Koenig hit .285. The team's weak links—and they were only weak comparatively—were Dugan at third and Collins behind the plate, and they batted .269 and .275 respectively.

The outfield was awesome. Ruth batted .356, broke his own record with 60 home runs, and drove in 164 runs. Meusel hit .337 and was the fourth man on the team to bat in more than 100 runs, with 103. Combs hit .356 and led the league with 23 triples. The team as a whole batted .307 and hit 158 home runs; no other team in the league hit more than 56, meaning that Ruth himself had outhomered every club in the league.

The pitching staff, already strong, was beefed up that year by Wilcy Moore, whom the Yankees had purchased from the Carolina League. Primarily a relief pitcher, Moore had one great year in the major leagues, and this was it; his record was 19–7. Dutch Ruether, a late-season acquisition from Washington the year before, and George Pipgras, recently brought up from the minors, were 13–6 and 10–3 respectively. Along with the newcomers were the usual stalwarts: Hoyt was 22–7, Pennock 19–8, Shocker 18–6. While the '27 Yankees are remembered mainly for their fireworks at home plate, one should bear in mind that this club also had superb pitching (the staff was the league leader in earned-run average).

Winning 110 games and losing 44 for a .714 percentage, Miller Huggins's team finished 19 games ahead of Connie Mack's Philadelphia Athletics, a team that was but two years away from its own run at greatness. This time there were no surprises in the World Series. As if to emphasize their greatness on the national stage, the Yankees steamrollered a good but overmatched Pittsburgh club in four straight.

In 1928, for the second time in the decade, the Yankees took a third consecutive pennant, their sixth in eight years. This time, however, their margin over the second-place Athletics was just 2½ games. Connie Mack's Lefty Grove–Mickey Cochrane–Jimmy Foxx–Al Simmons combine was just about ready, and the A's gave the champs a battle all season. On September 9, with the two teams in a virtual tie for first place, Mack brought his team into Yankee Stadium for a double-header. The Yankees swept them by scores of 3–0 and 7–3 and were never behind after that.

The '28 club simply wasn't as good as the '27 edition, despite some considerable thunder. Gehrig followed his .373 year with a .374 mark, but his home runs dropped from 47 to 27. Ruth had another great year, hitting 54 home runs, batting .323, and tying Gehrig with 142 runs batted in. But good as this was, each statistic was down from the year before. Combs and Meusel also had good seasons, but not quite as good as '27. Dugan's season was curtailed by an injury, and by the end of the year Joe had been waived to the Braves. Catching was a problem, but at the end of the season a twenty-one-year-old left-handed-hitting receiver named Bill Dickey was brought up from Little Rock for a brief look. Johnny Nee, one of the fine scouts the Yankees always managed to hire, had recommended Dickey, telling Barrow he would leave the profession forever if the youngster didn't make good.

Pipgras blossomed into a 24-game winner and Hoyt won 23. Pennock was 17–6 but suffered an arm injury and was never again the great pitcher he had been. A heart ailment had forced Shocker into retirement early in the season, and in September the Yankees were stunned to learn that the thirty-eight-year-old pitcher had died.

The Yankees were matched in the World Series

with their 1926 vanquishers, the St. Louis Cardinals. This time it was no contest; for the second year in a row, the New Yorkers swept the October festivities in four straight. It was a Ruth-Gehrig show, the slugging duo putting on the greatest two-man display in series history. Ruth batted .625, with three doubles and three home runs (all of his four-baggers coming in the fourth and final game). Gehrig went .545, smashing four homers and driving in nine runs in the four games.

The Yankees were a potent team, but in 1929 a more potent one, the Philadelphia Athletics, were ready to dominate, and they took the next three pennants. Ruth, Gehrig, Combs, and Lazzeri continued to hit, but the team was unable to replace Dugan at third. Koenig became erratic in the field and the Yankees tried a slick-fielding, light-hitting youngster named Leo Durocher at short. Meusel slipped badly and '29 was his last year in pinstripes. Young Dickey was a bright spot, catching 130 games and batting .324. The pitching staff was less effective, Pipgras being the ace with an 18–12 record. Hoyt and Pennock dropped to .500 records, and in another year Hoyt was gone.

The Yankee decade came to a close not only with disappointment but with tragedy as well; for the second time in two years the team was stunned by an untimely death. This time it was the manager, Miller Huggins. On September 20, 1929, Huggins, who seemed to have become more and more mentally and physically run-down as the season ran its course, entered a New York hospital with a case of blood poisoning. Five days later he was dead. For the first time in twelve years, the Yankees were looking for a manager.

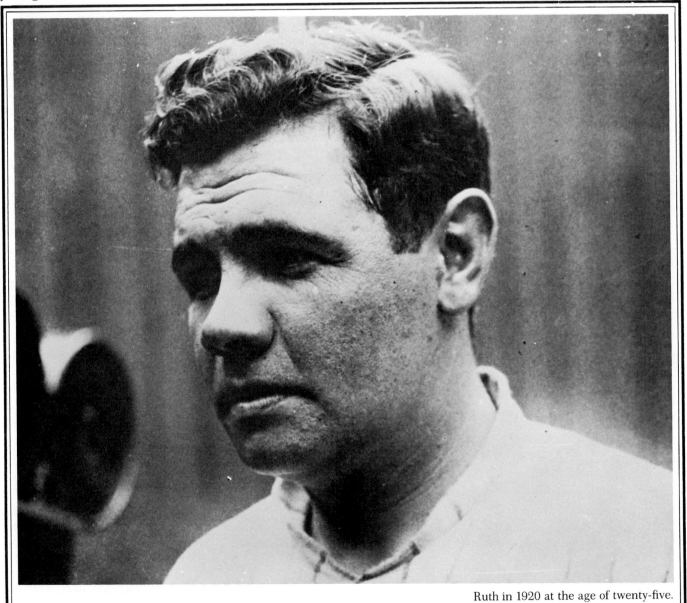

Ruth in 1920 at the age of twenty-five.

A trim young Babe Ruth in 1921.

Mike McNally was a utility man in the Yankee infield from 1921 to 1924, long enough to cash three World Series checks.

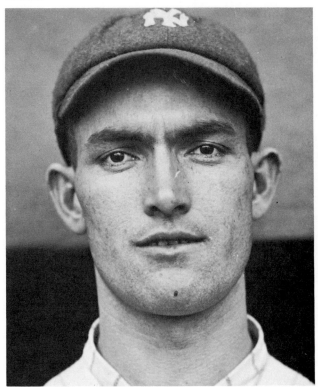

Home Run Baker in 1922. Baker played third for the Yankees from 1916 to 1922. He had his best year for them in 1918, when he batted .306.

Infielder Aaron Ward was with the Yankees from 1917 to 1926, much of the time as the club's regular second baseman. Steady in the field and with the bat, Ward's top season was 1921, when he batted .306.

A 1921 shot of Ruth staring intently out at the field.

Carl Mays, a cold, tough character and a big winner. Obtained from the Red Sox in midseason 1919 for two players and $40,000, he pitched for the Yankees from 1919 to 1923, with records of 26–11 and 27–9 in 1920 and 1921. He dropped to 13–14 in 1922; Huggins became disenchanted and waived Carl to Cincinnati after the 1923 season. In August 1920 he beaned Cleveland shortstop Ray Chapman at home plate in the Polo Grounds. Chapman died the following day from effects of the injury—major-league baseball's sole game-related fatality. Mays was accused of having thrown at Chapman, but this is unlikely. Chapman was notorious for crowding the plate; in fact, some of Mays's teammates say the fatal pitch may have been over the plate.

Ray Chapman. Cleveland's veteran shortstop was twenty-nine when he died.

Utility infielder Chick Fewster was with the Yankees from 1917 to 1922, batting .283 for a half-season's work in 1919.

Babe Ruth in 1921, the year he hit 59 home runs.

The Yankees' Bob Meusel and Giants manager John McGraw posing together during the 1921 World Series.

The third game of the 1921 World Series: Yankee Bob Meusel is out at home. The catcher is Frank Snyder, the umpire is Quigley.

Frank Frisch, a New York City native and a dynamic infielder for the Giants. He hit hard against the Yankees in the 1921, 1922, and 1923 World Series.

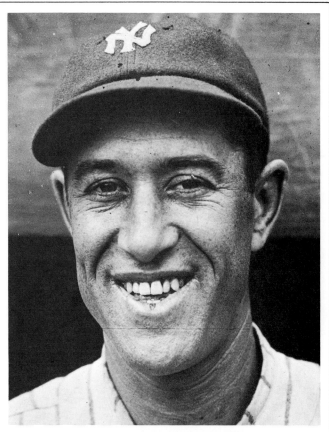

Emil ("Irish") Meusel, Bob's brother and one of McGraw's hard-hitting outfielders.

Bullet Joe Bush, the hard-throwing right-hander acquired from the Red Sox in December 1921 along with Sam Jones and Everett Scott in exchange for Roger Peckinpaugh, Jack Quinn, and two lesser lights. Joe pitched for the Yankees for three years and then was traded to the Browns for Urban Shocker. His best year in New York was 1922, when he was 26–7.

Everett Scott, Yankees shortstop from 1922 to 1925. His best year in pinstripes was '22, when he batted .269.

Bob Shawkey, an outstanding pitcher for the Yankees from 1915 to 1927. His top year was 1916, when he was 23–14.

Sam Jones, who pitched in the American League for twenty-two years. He was with the Yankees from 1922 to 1926, with a 21–8 record in 1923 his best effort.

Joe Bush.

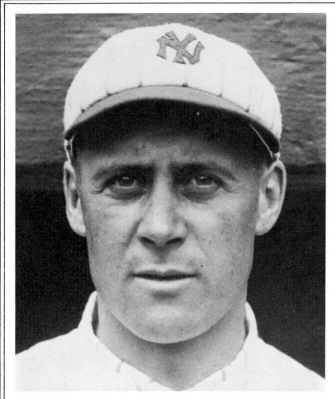

Wally Schang, who caught for the Yankees from 1921 to 1925. Probably the team's best catcher until Dickey, Wally's top years were .316 and .319 in 1921 and 1922.

His real name was Ladislaw Waldemar Wittkowski, but Yankee fans knew him as Whitey Witt. Whitey was in the Yankee outfield from 1922 to 1925, batting .314 in '23.

Miller Huggins and Jacob Ruppert just before the first game of the 1922 World Series.

The rival managers posing during the 1922 series—Miller Huggins (left) and the Giant's John McGraw.

McGraw and Ruth greeting each other during the 1922 series. As is apparent from this picture, they didn't much care for each other.

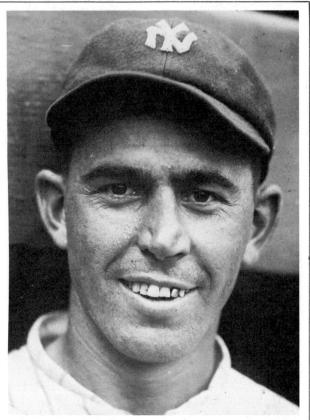

Fred Hofmann, Yankee back-up catcher from 1919 to 1925. His best effort was .290 in 72 games in 1923.

Bob Meusel, a heavy hitter with a powerful throwing arm, was in the Yankee outfield from 1920 to 1929. He hit over .300 seven times, with .337 in 1927 his high. In 1925 his 33 home runs and 138 runs batted in led the league. A taciturn man, he was known as "Silent Bob."

Elmer Smith, whom the Yankees obtained from Boston in 1922. The left-handed-hitting outfielder batted .306 as a part-timer in 1923 and then moved on.

Ed Barrow in 1920.

Joe Dugan, another acquisition from the Red Sox, played third base for the Yankees from 1922 to 1928. Between 1922 and 1926 Joe's averages were .287, .283, .302, .292, and .288; nice and steady.

Wally Schang is out at the plate in this 1923 game against the Browns at Yankee Stadium. Applying the tag is Browns catcher Hank Severeid.

The grand opening of Yankee Stadium, April 1923.

New York's Governor Al Smith is poised to throw out the first ball at the Stadium. Note that the upper stands in left field have not yet been built.

The Babe greeting the customers in 1923.

Casey Stengel in 1923.

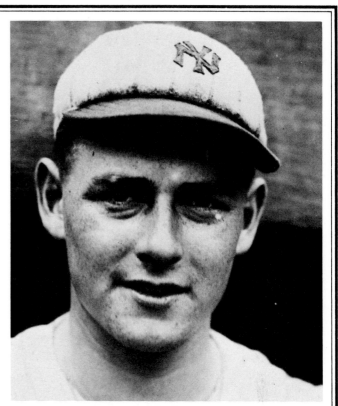

Herb Pennock, who pitched in the American League for twenty-two years. He was with the Yankees from 1923 to 1933. He was a control pitcher with an outstanding assortment of curve balls. Pennock had great years with the Yankees. In 1923 he was 19–6, in 1924 21–9, in 1926 23–11, in 1927 19–8, and in 1928 17–6. In World Series competition he was unbeaten, posting a 5–0 record.

Right-hander Waite ("Schoolboy") Hoyt, another long-time toiler in the big leagues. Hoyt pitched in the big time for twenty-one years, from 1921 to 1930 with the Yankees. He had many fine years for the club, once winning 17, once 18, and twice 19. His biggest years came back to back in 1927 and 1928, when he was 22–7 and 23–7.

The Babe finds himself in a bit of a jam in the second game of the 1923 series against the Giants. He had walked and then been picked off first by Giants catcher Frank Snyder. He is being run down by shortstop Dave Bancroft, who has just pitched the ball to first baseman George Kelly; Kelly is about to tag the great man out. Second baseman Frank Frisch is bringing up the rear and pitcher Jack Bentley has run over just in case. Earlier in the game Ruth had hit two home runs.

Opening day at Yankee Stadium, April 14, 1925, and the opposing managers are doing the traditional thing. The man Miller Huggins is glad-handing is Washington's player-manager Bucky Harris, who drove his team to a second consecutive pennant that year. In 1947 he won another, managing the Yankees.

(Below left)

Ben Paschal, reserve outfielder for the Yankees from 1924 to 1929. Playing 89 games in 1925, Ben, filling in for Ruth, swung a heavy stick, batting .360. He was a .300 hitter whenever he got the chance to play, but with outfield regulars named Ruth, Meusel, and Combs, that wasn't often.

(Below right)

Wally Pipp, Yankee first baseman from 1915 to 1925. The left-handed-hitting Pipp twice led the league in home runs and once in triples, twice driving in over 100 runs. His best year was .329 in 1922. Then one day he sat down and the Yanks put in young Gehrig, and soon Wally found himself in Cincinnati.

Lou Gehrig in 1927.

The Yankees' young keystone duo in 1926: shortstop Mark Koenig (left) and second baseman Tony Lazzeri.

Benny Bengough, Yankees catcher from 1923 to 1930. Benny, a lifetime .250 hitter, was usually kept in reserve.

For more than forty years, in an almost unbroken span of time, the Yankees had a Hall of Famer in center field. The first was Earle Combs, shown here in 1926. Joining the team in 1924, Combs became a regular the next year and remained until 1935, a year before the arrival of DiMaggio. In his twelve-year career, all of it spent in New York, Combs batted .325.

Miller Huggins in 1925.

Three men and their shadows. Bob Meusel is out at home in the first inning of game four of the 1926 World Series at Sportsman's Park in St. Louis. Meusel was trying to score from first on a single by Gehrig. Bob O'Farrell is the catcher, Bill Klem the umpire.

Gehrig coming to bat at Yankee Stadium during the 1926 series.

Relief ace Wilcy Moore, a pleasant surprise in 1927 with a 19–7 record. He was unable to recapture that magic, however, with 4–4 and 6–4 records the next two years, and was dealt away. He returned to the Yankees in 1932 and 1933 and again pitched ineffectually.

Getting ready.

Huggins and Ruth in 1927.

The Cardinals' Jesse Haines, whose departure from the game set up the classic confrontation between Alexander and Lazzeri in game seven of the 1926 World Series.

Tony Lazzeri, the Yankees' all-time second baseman, is remembered primarily for striking out against Alexander. This is unfair, because Tony, who played for the Yankees from 1926 to 1937, was an outstanding performer. He batted over .300 five times, with a high of .354 in 1929, and seven times drove in over 100 runs.

Grover Cleveland Alexander as he looked at the time of the Lazzeri strikeout.

Rogers Hornsby, player-manager of the 1926 St. Louis Cardinals.

The Babe about to unload.

George Pipgras, a hard-throwing right-hander who pitched for the Yankees from 1923 to 1924 and from 1927 to 1933. His top year was '28, when he was 24–13. The following year he was 18–12. In 1933 he was traded to the Red Sox and soon after broke his arm while snapping off a curve, ending his career. The Red Sox never had any luck trading with the Yankees.

Earle Combs.

Herb Pennock.

Ruth being greeted at home plate by Gehrig after hitting his 60th home run of the season on September 30, 1927, at Yankee Stadium.

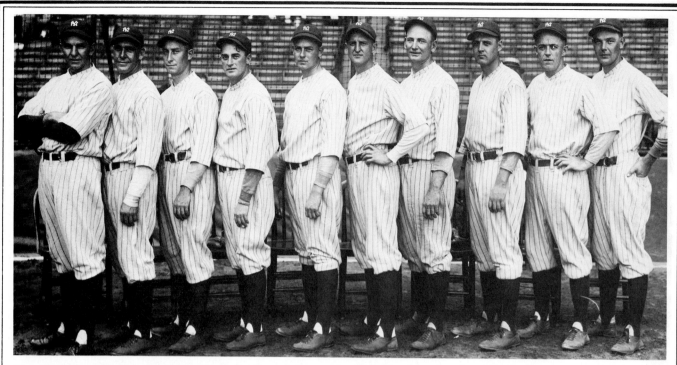

The pitching staff of the 1927 New York Yankees. Left to right: Bob Shawkey, Joe Giard, Myles Thomas, Urban Shocker, Waite Hoyt, Herb Pennock, Wilcy Moore, Walter Beall, Dutch Reuther, George Pipgras. Beall pitched in only one game; Giard was in sixteen games and had no decisions, and Shawkey was about through; in effect, it was pretty much a seven-man staff.

The infield of the 1927 New York Yankees. Left to right: Lou Gehrig, Tony Lazzeri, Mark Koenig, Joe Dugan.

Babe Ruth.

The eighth inning of the second game of the 1927 World Series at Pittsburgh. The Yankees' Bob Meusel has just scored on a wild pitch delivered by Pirate pitcher Vic Aldridge, who has come down to cover the plate. The catcher is Johnny Gooch and the batter falling away from the action is Joe Dugan.

Henry ("Hank") Johnson, a right-hander who pitched for the Yankees from 1925 to 1932 (excluding 1927). Hank, who was fast but wild, had his best season in 1928, when he was 14–9.

Colonel Ruppert giving five to the Washington Senators' great pitcher Walter Johnson.

Two sluggers from the golden age: heavyweight champ Jack Dempsey and home-run champ Babe Ruth.

Aerial view of Yankee Stadium in 1928. The Yankees are playing Connie Mack's A's and the place is sold out.

The joint is jumping in St. Louis in the eighth inning of the fourth and final game of the 1928 World Series. Ruth has just stepped on home plate after popping his third home run of the game and the crowd, forgetting that they're supposed to be rooting for the Cardinals, have tossed their straw skimmers onto the field in delight.

Walter ("Dutch") Ruether joined the Yankees at the tag end of a fine career, pitching for the New Yorkers in 1926 and 1927. He was 13–6 in '27, his last year in the big leagues.

Pat Collins, Yankees catcher for three pennant-winning years, 1926–1928. Pat's best was in 1926, when he batted .286.

Miller Huggins.

Mark Koenig in 1926, his first full season with the Yankees. Mark was the regular shortstop until early in the 1930 season, when he was traded to Detroit. His best year was 1928, when he batted .319.

Urban Shocker, in 1926, two years before his death.

Right-hander Myles Thomas pitched for the Yankees from 1926 to 1929, much of the time coming out of the bullpen. His most effective season was 1927, when he was 7–4.

Cedric Durst was an outfield reserve for the Yankees from 1927 to 1930, playing infrequently and with modest success. Durst's place in Yankee history is secure, however, as the man they traded to the Red Sox for Red Ruffing.

The Babe again, saddled up on a bucking automobile at Dexter Park in Brooklyn in October 1928. Ruth and Gehrig (yes, that's Lou on the left) were beginning a postseason barnstorming tour and advertising the coming rodeo at the same time. As always, the crowds had come out to see him.

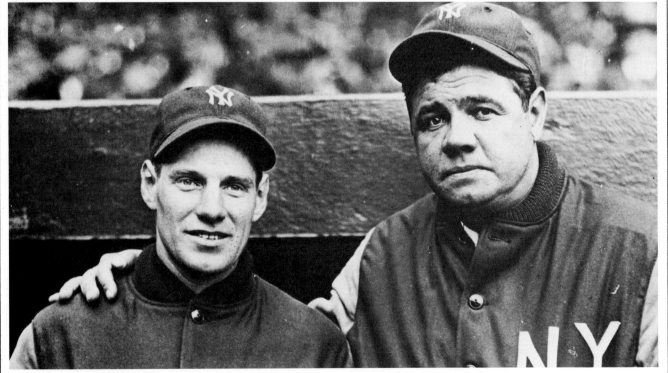

Ruth and rookie infielder Leo Durocher in 1929; Ruth looks as though he has doubled in size since joining the Yankees nine years earlier. Leo came up the year before and batted .270. In '29 he slipped to .246 and was waived to Cincinnati after the season. Only twenty-four at the time, he had a long career of controversy, excitement, and glory ahead of him.

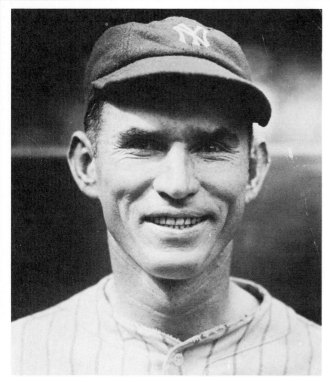

Tom Zachary pitched for the Yankees from the end of 1928 to the beginning of 1930. The veteran lefty holds two distinctions: he gave up Ruth's 60th home run in 1927, and in 1929 he had a perfect 12–0 record, which remains the high-water mark for games won in a season without a loss.

Connie Mack, whose Philadelphia Athletics broke the Yankees' dominance of the American League in 1929.

Lou Gehrig slashing away in 1929.

Joe McCarthy, manager of the Chicago Cubs, in 1929.

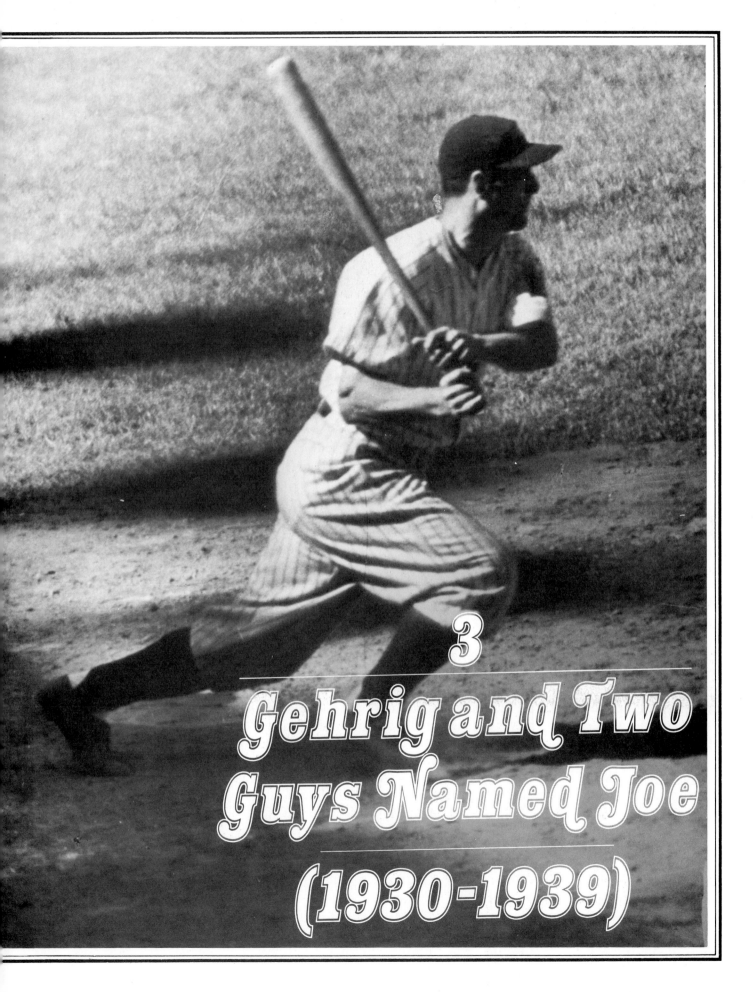

3
Gehrig and Two
Guys Named Joe
(1930-1939)

Ruth thought he should be the next manager of the Yankees. As time went on, managing became a fixation of his. He was never given the opportunity and he never understood why. As far as baseball people were concerned, the reason was simple: how could he expect to manage others when he was unable to manage himself? It was not exactly a couple of romantics who ran the Yankees in those years; Ruppert and Barrow were a pair of hardheaded pragmatists.

In 1930, the man they chose to succeed Huggins was Bob Shawkey, whose fine pitching career had come to a close in 1927. On the surface Shawkey seemed a good choice. He was a likable man and possessed good baseball sense. He was, however, handed a difficult assignment, not the least of which was replacing a highly respected and successful manager.

It proved a transitional year for the Yankees. While the Athletics stormed through the league winning their second straight flag, the New Yorkers tried to rebuild. Shawkey and Hoyt had some disagreements, and early in the season Hoyt was traded to Detroit along with Koenig. The left side of the infield was manned by a couple of youngsters, Lyn Lary at short and Ben Chapman at third. Chapman switched to the outfield the next year and remained with the Yankees until 1935. He was a .300 hitter, a blazing base stealer, and a difficult character. It was Ben who in 1934 reportedly told an aging Ruth, "If I were as old as you are, and as rich as you are, I wouldn't risk my health by playing anymore." History has not recorded Ruth's response.

The club continued to hit—their .309 average is the highest in Yankee history—and attendance was strong. For the ninth time in 11 years they drew over a million, an impressive record when one realizes that with the exception of the 1924 Tigers no other American League team had as yet drawn a million customers.

The problem lay on the mound. Hoyt was gone, Pennock fading, and Pipgras had become a .500 pitcher. There was, however, a whiff of old times in the air. Early in the season the Yankees had an opportunity to obtain a pitcher from their old trading mates, the Red Sox. The choice lay between three right-handers: Ed Morris, a fairly good pitcher; Danny MacFayden, a respectable winner for the lowly Sox; and Charley (Red) Ruffing, a hard thrower whose chief distinction thus far had been leading the league in losses in 1928 and 1929. The shrewd Shawkey told Barrow to get Ruffing.

Shawkey had spotted what he felt was a minor flaw in Ruffing's delivery and felt that with a little work Charley could be straightened out. The club took Shawkey's advice, and for $50,000 and utility outfielder Cedric Durst they obtained one of their greatest pitchers. Ruffing was 15–5 in his first year in pinstripes.

Toward the end of the season, Shawkey, who had been given a one-year contract, began asking Ruppert about next year. Jake said they would talk about it after the season, assuring his skipper that this was the way they always did it with Hug. One day soon after the season had ended, Shawkey went up to the Yankee office to talk over some business. "I was heading for Barrow's office," Shawkey recalled years later, "when the door opened and Joe McCarthy came walking out. I took one look and turned around and got out of there. I knew what had happened."

"I never played in the big leagues," Joe McCarthy once said. "Not one game. Wasn't good enough, I guess. But I think I spent more time trying to get up there than almost anybody I know of. I was twenty years in the minor leagues, as player and manager, before I made it." He made it in 1926, as manager of the Chicago Cubs. He moved his team steadily forward, finally winning the pennant in 1929. (Over a twenty-four-year managerial career, no McCarthy-led team ever finished lower than fourth.) After finishing second in 1930, Joe was canned by the Cubs. The Yankees, always with a sharp eye for talent whether on the field, in the front office, or among the scouting ranks, wasted no time in signing up the forty-three-year-old Philadelphia-born Irishman.

Joseph Vincent McCarthy became the epitome of the Yankee manager. He was shrewd, serious, all business, and not without some twinkling Irish wit. His players were awed by his baseball knowledge, and his prodigious memory. "He never made notes," one of his players said years later. "He didn't have to. He never forgot anything."

Ruth bitterly resented McCarthy's appointment. To the Babe it seemed all wrong. The chief wrong, of course, was in not hiring the Babe himself. There was also the fact that McCarthy was a National Leaguer. And on top of that the final insult—the man had never played a day in the big leagues.

McCarthy recognized the Ruth problem and he handled it with consummate skill—by ignoring it. Ruth was thirty-six years old and McCarthy knew that in a few years the problem would take care of itself. Ruth, who had learned not to butt heads with either front office or managerial authority, was unhappy, but as always he gave 100 percent on the field.

The new manager recognized that there was something special about being a Yankee. He insisted his men turn out in jackets and ties when on the road, and he cut out the card playing in the clubhouse. The Yankee image of businesslike efficiency was polished by McCarthy, as was the Yankee tradition of pride and winning that was passed from player to player and from team to team.

McCarthy could handle many things, but not the Philadelphia Athletics in 1931. Connie Mack's last great team swept to their third straight pennant rather handily, outdistancing the second-place Yankees by 13½ games, led by Lefty Grove's 31–4 record and Al Simmons's .390 batting average.

Gehrig, in full bloom now, set an American League record with 184 runs batted in, and tied Ruth for the home-run lead with 46, the only time except for Ruth's last year that the Crown Prince was able to match the Sultan in home runs. The aging Babe gave McCarthy the last of his superhuman years, with a .373 average and 163 runs batted in.

A twenty-two-year-old rookie left-hander named Vernon ("Lefty") Gomez exploded on the scene for the New Yorkers with a 21–9 record. The hard-throwing Gomez was an engaging character, one of the purest wits ever to play big-league ball. When asked how far into Yankee Stadium's upper-left-field stands one of Jimmy Foxx's mammoth home runs had sent a Gomez fast ball, Lefty said, "I don't know how far it went, but I do know it takes forty-five minutes to walk up there." Gomez once told a young pitcher how to play a line drive that was hit straight back at him: "Run in on it." And it was Gomez who responded to a questioner by attributing his success to "clean living and a fast outfield."

For the Yankees, 1932 turned out to be an unexpectedly easy year. Winning 107 games, they outclassed the Athletics by 13 games. Gomez, a full-fledged star now, was 24–7, Ruffing 18–7, Pipgras 16–9. The team also got a 17–4 season out of a tempestuous, hard-throwing rookie right-hander named Johnny Allen.

At shortstop the Yankees had Frank Crosetti, whom they had purchased from the San Francisco Seals of the Pacific Coast League. Veteran Joe Sewell, obtained from Cleveland the year before, was at third. Sewell, the most difficult man in baseball history to strike out, displayed his specialty for New York fans that year, fanning just three times in 503 at bats. Years later, when an intrepid interviewer asked Joe for the secret behind his uncanny ability to make contact, Sewell confided, "You have to keep your eye on the ball."

It was in 1932 that Gehrig and Ruth had their most memorable days on a baseball diamond. For Lou it came on June 3, at Philadelphia's Shibe Park. In that game he became the first man in the twentieth century to hit four home runs in one game, hitting them consecutively. It is one of baseball's oft-told tales that Gehrig was overshadowed throughout his career, first by Ruth and later by DiMaggio. It was no different on his greatest day, for on that same June 3 John McGraw decided to step down as the Giants' manager after 31 years. John J. got the headlines and Lou got another line in the record book.

Typically, Ruth saved his moment for the big stage—the World Series. It was a bitter series against McCarthy's former team, the Cubs. The bench jockeying, an art form in those years, was particularly sulfurous. What provoked the ill-feeling was what the Yankees considered the shabby treatment afforded an old friend, Mark Koenig. When the Cubs' regular shortstop, Billy Jurges, suffered a late-season injury, the team picked up Koenig, whose play was superb down the stretch. He fielded well and batted .353 in his 33 games, making a strong contribution to the Cubs' hard-fought victory over Pittsburgh. The Cubs then voted Koenig but a half-share of their series loot. This offended the Yankees and galled Ruth in particular, the Babe being one of the Western world's big spenders. Ruth let the Cubs know in no uncertain terms what he thought of their niggardly treatment of his old buddy. The insults flew back and forth, growing in both heat and volume. Not helpful to the Cubs' dispositions was the bombing the Yankee bats gave them in the first two games. That set the stage for game three.

In the top of the fifth inning, the score was tied 4–4. On the mound for the Cubs was a tough right-hander, Charlie Root. At the plate was Babe Ruth. The noise coming from the Chicago dugout, all of it aimed at Ruth, was replete with indelicacies. Root poured in two strikes. Ruth stepped out. What next occurred has been, and always will be, a matter of controversy and conjecture. Ruth made a pointing gesture—at whom, to where, why, is uncertain. Some said it was at Root, some say it was toward the Cub bench, some say it was at the center-field bleachers. There is no question about what he did on the next pitch—he hit a tremendous home run into those bleachers, the longest home run, it was said at the time, ever hit in Chicago's Wrigley Field.

The legend of the "called shot" developed later. Someone suggested to Ruth after the game that he had called the home run. Babe, ever the showman, went along with it. The public loved it and it became part of baseball folklore.

Did he or didn't he? Many Yankee players said yes; many Cub players said no. Joe McCarthy, who missed very little of what took place on a ball field, said, "Tell you the truth, I didn't see him point anywhere at all. But maybe I turned my head for a moment." Years later Ruth and Root happened to come together in Hollywood on the set of the movie *Pride of the Yankees*, being filmed just after Gehrig's death. With them was the old Brooklyn Dodger slugger Babe Herman, who portrayed Gehrig at the plate in the movie's long shots. After some conversation, Root, according to Herman, said, "Say, Babe, you didn't really call your shot that day, did you?" Ruth laughed, and said, "Of course not. But it made a hell of a story, didn't it?"

Not even Babe's own testimony can alter what the myth makers have wrought and the believers choose to believe. George Washington chopped down his cherry tree, and Babe Ruth called his shot. And that's that.

Ruth got the headlines in the '32 series, and Gehrig, who batted .529, hit three home runs, and drove in eight runs in the four-game sweep, was overshadowed. Bill Dickey, by now running neck and neck with Mickey Cochrane as the game's premier catcher, batted .438. It was the Yankees' third four-game sweep in a row, coming after the '27 and '28 mashings they had given Pittsburgh and St. Louis.

The very impressive 1932 season did not, however, launch another clutch of pennants, which is the way Yankee teams have traditionally won them. Only twice in their 32 championship seasons—in 1932 and 1947—did the team fail to repeat. Otherwise their flags have come, like plagues upon the rest of the American League, in threes, fours, and fives.

In 1933 the Washington Senators won the pennant and the Yankees finished second, seven games out. Ruth, going downhill noticeably, batted .301 with 34 home runs, second in the league to Jimmy Foxx's 48. The aging slugger had now become more of a liability than an asset, although the fans were still pouring in to see him, even in that Depression year. Attendance was down, but the Yankees' draw of 728,000 was far and away the best in baseball.

The New Yorkers remained in second place for the next two years as the Detroit Tigers captured a pair of pennants. Detroit's win in 1934 broke what had been the league's eastern division's curious grip on American League pennants; the last western division winner had been Cleveland in 1920.

Nineteen thirty-four was, to the relief of the Yankees, Ruth's last year. After again petitioning for McCarthy's job and being told it was not available, Babe Ruth left the Yankees. Not wanting to offend the great man's vast public by simply turning him loose, Ruppert and Barrow quietly worked out a rather complex deal with the Boston Braves, a half-dead franchise. Hoping Ruth's magic would hype the gate, the Braves signed him to a contract whereby Babe became a vice-president, assistant manager to Bill McKechnie, and, of course, a player. It sounded rather impressive, but in the end it amounted to virtually nothing.

Ruth remained with the Braves until June and then retired, leaving behind a .181 batting average. A few days before he quit, however, he unleashed one last mighty performance, hitting three long home runs in spacious Forbes Field in Pittsburgh.

The unenviable job of replacing Ruth in right field was given to newcomer George Selkirk, dubbed "Twinkletoes" because of his odd way of running. Unfairly booed at first by some of Ruth's diehard fans, Selkirk gave the Yankees a half-dozen years of solid service, hitting over .300 five times and twice driving in more than 100 runs.

Another new face in the big Bronx ball park belonged to Robert ("Red") Rolfe. Rolfe came to the Yankees in '34 as a shortstop. With Crosetti firmly entrenched at that position, McCarthy moved the line-drive-hitting Rolfe to third, where Red settled in for the next eight years. With Gehrig at first and the veteran Lazzeri playing well and hitting hard at second, the Yankees had their first fixed infield in quite a while.

McCarthy's problems were in the outfield, particularly center field. Combs had worn down to a part-timer and retired after the '35 season, and the fiery Chapman had finally worn down McCarthy's patience. Rid of his Ruth headache, Joe was not about to brook nonsense from a mere mortal, and Ben was soon exiled to Washington in exchange for outfielder Jake Powell.

Another problem child, Johnny Allen, was traded to Cleveland after the 1935 season for right-handers Monte Pearson and Steve Sundra. Gomez and Ruffing were still at the top of the staff (Lefty had dazzled the league with a 26–5 record in '34), and McCarthy had come up with a fine relief pitcher, Johnny Murphy, a curve-balling righty with what sports writers liked to describe as "a map-of-Ireland face."

McCarthy felt that 1936 would be the year to topple the high-riding Tigers and reclaim the pennant if only the Yankees could add the outfielder they needed. They did just that. As a matter of fact, they had already owned him for more than a year.

In 1933 the most exciting minor-league player in the country was an eighteen-year-old outfielder playing for the San Francisco Seals, Joseph Paul DiMaggio. Born to excel on a baseball diamond, DiMaggio brought to his performances a grace and purity that served to enhance the gifts that were already astonishing in their abundance. In the 1940s a phrase was coined to describe the ring talents of boxer Sugar Ray Robinson: "Pound for pound the greatest fighter of all time." One might adjust this description to fit DiMaggio: "Inning for inning the greatest baseball player of all time." When he wasn't hitting baseballs with the wickedest right-handed swing since Hornsby's, he was covering the vast Yankee center field with a thoroughbred's strides, taking balls out of the air with absurd ease and, when necessary, firing the same kinds of line drives he hit.

He was the perfect player. He was also the perfect Yankee, for he brought with him the kind of cool, aloof pride in self and performance that were becoming Yankee trademarks. Fans and sports writers could not quite determine whether he was aloof, shy, or something of a snob. But of one thing there never was any doubt: he possessed in his quiet way the same on-field as well as off-field magic that Ruth did, mesmerizing the public with his undemonstrative personality as surely as Ruth had with his totally uninhibited ways. His teammates worshiped DiMaggio, his opponents admired and respected him. Decades after his retirement he moved through ball parks like a king through corners of his realm, receiving adulation he never demanded but which baseball fans felt it natural to accord.

In 1933 the youngster batted a power-laden .340 for San Francisco (a city not far from where he had grown up, eighth of nine children of an Italian immigrant fisherman). What captured the attention of the baseball world, however, was the 61-game hitting streak he put together. The Seals, naturally, were inundated with offers for their precocious star. But the Seals management decided to hold onto DiMaggio for another season, in anticipation of his improving and thus commanding even more money on the open market.

One night during the 1934 season DiMaggio injured his knee getting out of a taxi, and it looked as though the Seals had outsmarted themselves. Another injury soon after sidelined him for the season, and the $75,000 tag the Seals had placed on him looked like wishful thinking. All the interested teams backed off—except one.

Two Yankee scouts, Joe Devine and Bill Essick, implored Barrow to buy the youngster. Barrow, who hired intelligent men because he trusted their judgment, agreed (but only after DiMaggio's knee received an okay from an orthopedist selected by the Yankees). The Seals were asking $40,000, but Barrow bargained them down to twenty-five grand and five minor-league players. As part of the deal the Yankees agreed to let Joe play another year in San Francisco. To the chagrin of the big-league clubs which had been unwilling to gamble on the youngster, DiMaggio played a full, unhampered season and batted .398.

With the arrival of Joe DiMaggio in 1936, the Yankee success story assumed dynastic proportions: beginning with what would eventually be known as the DiMaggio era, the Yankees won an astonishing 22 pennants in 29 years. The 1936 Yankees, with twenty-one-year-old DiMaggio in center field, were a machine nearly as awesome as the club's 1927 edition. The '27 team won more games (110 to 102) and batted higher (.307 to .300), but otherwise they were outgunned in virtually every other department by the '36 club.

The two holdovers from '27, Gehrig and Lazzeri, were still performing well; Lou hit a career-high 49 home runs and was setting an endurance record every time he started another game. Crosetti hit a personal high of .288 that year, while Rolfe, Selkirk, Powell, Dickey, Gehrig, and DiMaggio all hit over .300. Five men—Gehrig, Lazzeri, Dickey, Selkirk, and DiMaggio—drove in more than 100 runs each, setting a major-league record that still stands. Dickey's .362 batting average remains the highest ever for a catcher. The rookie DiMaggio batted .323 and hit 29 home runs. (It was a memorable year for rookies; Cleveland introduced their seventeen-year-old fireballing right-hander Bob Feller that season.) Ruffing led the pitchers with 20 wins, followed by Pearson's 19, and winning seasons were enjoyed by Bump Hadley (recently acquired from Washington), Gomez, Johnny Broaca, Pat Malone, and Murphy.

Once again, as it had been in the early 1920s, New York City was the baseball capital of the world, with the Giants winning the National League pennant. Averaging better than seven runs a game, the Yankees won the series in six. A defeat at the hands of the Giants' great left-hander Carl Hubbell in the opener broke the Yanks' 12-game World Series winning streak.

In 1937 it was almost as easy, with another 102 victories and a 13-game margin over second-place Detroit. Nothing was going to stop those Yankee teams; with Selkirk out much of the year with a broken collarbone and Powell sidelined because of illness, the team found outfield replacements in Myril Hoag, who hit .301, and a twenty-four-year-old who was to become one of the most popular Yankees, Tommy Henrich. In 67 games the left-handed-hitting Henrich batted .320, an auspicious beginning to a fine career, during which he became known as "Old Reliable" in tribute to his clutch hitting.

Henrich had been signed as a free agent for $25,000 after being turned loose from the Cleveland organization by Judge Landis, who disapproved of the way the Indians were manipulating Henrich's career by denying the hard-hitting youngster a chance in the big leagues. Henrich was offered more money by other teams, but it was with the Yankees, baseball's glamor team, that he wanted to play. "I'd been a Yankee fan since I was eight years old," Henrich said. "I was a Babe Ruth man." Ruth, although gone three years, was still the embodiment of the Yankee magic. That vast stadium was still his, the grass in right field still pulsated with his presence, and that was where all the bright young players in the land wanted to be.

Gehrig, just two years away from sudden, tragic retirement, was swinging with undiminished might, batting .351, hitting 37 home runs, and knocking in 159 runs. But it was a DiMaggio team now; Joe hit 46 home runs that year, an incredible total for a right-handed hitter in the Stadium. He batted .346 and drove in 167 runs. Dickey batted .332 with 29 homers and 133 runs batted in, still the American League record for catchers. Gomez was 21–11 and Ruffing 20–7, with Lefty leading the league in earned-run average and shutouts.

For the second year in a row, the Yankees met the Giants in the World Series, and this time they vanquished their old rivals in five games. Gomez, who had won two games in the '36 series, did the same in '37, running his lifetime World Series record to 5–0.

Lazzeri led the Yankees at bat that October with a .400 average. It proved to be a last hurrah for the veteran second baseman; despite his fine series, Tony's average had dropped to .244 in 1937, and a few days after the series the Yankees gave him his unconditional release. Tony signed on with the Cubs and wound up in the 1938 series against his old mates.

It was not just Lazzeri's batting average that persuaded the Yankees to let the veteran go; the bigger reason was named Joe Gordon, a twenty-two-year-old second baseman who had just finished a fine year playing for the Yankees' Newark farm team in the International League. Gordon had originally been signed as a shortstop, but McCarthy converted him to second base. A right-handed hitter with good power, Gordon showed Yankee fans some of the flashiest fielding around second base that they had seen in a long time.

The 1938 Yankees won their third straight pennant by 9½ games over the Red Sox. Rookie Joe Gordon batted .255, but it was a lethal .255, with 25 home runs and 97 runs batted in. Henrich, now a regular in the outfield, drove in 91 runs, with 22 homers. DiMaggio hit .324 and drove in 140. Dickey, that catcher who hit like an outfielder, batted .313, hitting 27 homers and collecting 115 runs batted in. Ruffing topped the staff with a 21–7 record, his third straight 20-game season. Behind him was Gomez with an 18–12 record and Pearson with 16–7, followed by newcomer Spud Chandler's 14–5.

By season's end Gehrig had played in 2,122 consecutive games. Lou's year was a good one by normal standards but a poor one by his own. His .295 average was his lowest since his rookie year of 1926, his 29 homers his lowest since 1928, his 114 RBIs his lowest since '26. Lou was thirty-five years old and people assumed that the "Iron Horse" was simply beginning to yield to age; no one suspected that it could be something more.

There was some drama but little suspense in the 1938 World Series against the Cubs. The Yankees were an unstoppable steamroller, and they flattened the Cubs in four straight, as they had done in 1932, but this time without the vitriol.

The drama came in game two, when the Cubs started a lame-armed Dizzy Dean. Dean, who just a few years before had been baseball's greatest pitcher and, after Ruth's retirement, its biggest drawing card, had lost his flaming speed to an injury and was getting by on guts and guile. He had slow-curved the Yankees into submission for seven innings, carrying a 3–2 lead into the eighth. But then Crosetti tagged him for a home run with a man on, and an inning later DiMaggio did the same. Like Ruth, who could excite the crowd by striking out, Dean possessed the kind of magnetism that made him the center of attention even in defeat.

The Cubs went quietly in four, bowing twice to Ruffing and once each to Pearson and Gomez. Lefty ran his World Series history to 6–0, where it remained, the most glittering pitching record in series play.

The year 1939 would be one of mixed emotions for the Yankees. On January 13, Jacob Ruppert died in a New York hospital at the age of seventy-two. Control of the team passed into the hands of the Ruppert estate, with Ed Barrow moving up as president, in charge of all operations.

Gehrig worked hard all winter, wanting to be in shape for spring training at St. Petersburg and to atone for his "off" year. But the hard work—and no one was ever a harder or more dedicated worker—did not seem to pay off. The snap was gone from the powerful swing, and when he did get wood on the ball his shots were going to left field. His fielding was sluggish; his reflexes were slow. When he tried to run all-out he looked, as someone remarked, "like a man running in sand."

"The fellows would laugh and kid him," teammate Wes Ferrell recalled of that spring. They accused him of getting old. It was good-natured, roughhouse baseball humor.

One day some of the players went to the golf course to watch the professionals in the St. Petersburg Open. "I noticed Lou," Ferrell said, "walking all by himself along the edge of the woods. I watched him for a while and noticed something peculiar. Instead of wearing cleats, which normally he would have worn for walking across the grass, he was wearing tennis sneakers and was *sliding* his feet as he went along, instead of picking them up and putting them down. Looking back now, I realize why. His muscles were so deteriorated that just the effort of lifting his feet a few inches to walk had already become too much."

Gehrig opened the season at first base. He added eight more games to his remarkable streak and showed a puny .143 batting average—four singles in 28 at bats.

McCarthy, who knew that something was radically wrong with his great star, said nothing, refusing to bench Gehrig. Years later, near the end of his long life, McCarthy was showing a writer around his house outside of Buffalo, New York. The walls were adorned with framed pictures of the Yankee championship teams, as well as individual photographs of some of the greatest stars—Ruth, Gehrig, DiMaggio, Dickey, etc. Going to the living room, the writer noticed a single framed picture on a small table. It was of Gehrig, autographed to McCarthy and his wife. "Two pictures of Gehrig," McCarthy said with a smile. "I guess you might think he was my favorite, eh?" he added, with a sly wink of the eye.

In the spring of 1939 McCarthy was leaving it up to Lou. The end came on May 2, in Detroit. In a conversation with McCarthy in the skipper's hotel room the night before, Gehrig had asked to be taken out of the lineup. McCarthy agreed it was the right thing to do.

"I knew there was something wrong with him," McCarthy said, "but I didn't know what it was. His reflexes were shot. I was afraid of his getting hit with a pitched ball. That was my chief concern, to get him out of there before he was hurt."

Not long after, Gehrig went to the Mayo Clinic in Rochester, Minnesota. Tests revealed that he was suffering from a rare neuromuscular disease, amyotrophic lateral sclerosis, which gradually atrophied the muscles, slowly causing them to cease functioning. There was—and is—no cure.

On July 4, more than 60,000 fans filled Yankee Stadium for Lou Gehrig Appreciation Day. Between games of a double-header with the Washington Senators there were speeches, tributes, gifts. Thirteen members of the 1927 Yankees were in attendance. A visibly affected Gehrig finally went to the microphone and made a short, simple, eloquent speech. He may have been given a bad break, he said, "Yet today I consider myself the luckiest man on the face of the earth." Two years later, on June 2, 1941, Gehrig died, a few weeks short of his thirty-eighth birthday.

Ellsworth ("Babe") Dahlgren, a journeyman ballplayer who played competently but unspectacularly for eight clubs in a twelve-year major-league career, will always be remembered as the man who replaced Lou Gehrig. Dahlgren was the Yankees' first baseman for two years, showing some power but batting only .235 and .264.

In spite of the loss of their great slugger and field captain, the Yankees shattered the league in 1939, winning 106 games and finishing 17 ahead of the Red Sox. Ruffing logged another 21–7 record, his fourth 20-game season in a row. Gomez, beginning to slip, was 12–8. McCarthy, with a plethora of pitchers, used them all, so that in spite of the club's 106 victories only Ruffing won more than 13. Newcomer Atley Donald was 13–3, Hadley 12–6, Pearson 12–5, Sundra 11–1, Oral Hildebrand (obtained from the Browns) 10–4, and rookie left-hander Marius Russo 8–3.

DiMaggio, after challenging .400 for much of the year, settled for what was to be his highest batting average, a league-leading .381. Rookie Charlie Keller took over in left field and added another potent bat to an already smoking lineup, hitting .334. Keller, a fierce-looking but gentle man with bulging biceps, was nicknamed "King Kong." After sizing up his new teammate for the first time, Gomez said, referring to the famous big-game hunter, "Frank Buck brought him back alive." With Selkirk hitting over .300 and driving in more than 100 runs, there was so much talent in the outfield that Henrich was temporarily reduced to a part-time player.

When someone asked Frank McCormick years later about the 1939 World Series, the former Cincinnati first baseman smiled and said, "What World Series?" Despite the presence on the Cincinnati pitching staff of the National League's two mightiest pitchers, 27-game winner Bucky Walters and 25-game winner Paul Derringer, the Yanks achieved the fifth four-game sweep in their history (out of six four-game sweeps in series play, the Yankees had five; the other belonged to the 1914 Boston Braves).

Ruffing outpitched Derringer in the Stadium opener 2–1, the run crossing in the last of the ninth. The next day Pearson hurled one of the finest games in series history, two-hitting the Reds 4–0. Monte had a no-hitter until Ernie Lombardi singled with one out in the eighth; the Reds got another hit in the ninth.

The series moved to Cincinnati and the New Yorkers took game three. In game four their sweep was in jeopardy, but two runs in the ninth tied the score. They broke it open in the tenth; with Crosetti and Keller on base, DiMaggio singled in one run. When there was some loose play in the outfield Keller also came home. The onrushing Keller crashed into Lombardi at the plate, stunning the big catcher and jarring loose the ball. As the dazed Lombardi sat on the ground, the ball a few feet away, the alert DiMaggio never broke stride and came in to score. They called it "Lombardi's snooze," which was unfair to the great Cincinnati catcher, who had been knocked almost unconscious by the collision. Besides, the winning runs were already in when Ernie was spilled.

The Yankees had achieved something unprecedented in baseball history—four consecutive pennants and four consecutive world championships. From various corners of the baseball world the cry came: "Break up the Yankees." From Cincinnati came a plaintive voice: "Never mind the Yankees; break up Keller." The rookie had torn the Reds apart almost single-handedly in the four games, batting .438 with three home runs, a triple, a double, and six runs batted in.

The Yankees had absorbed the loss of Gehrig and gone on. They were a young team, strong and powerful, with an abundance of good pitching. It looked like only old age could stop them.

The year is 1930, and this twelve-year-old denizen of New York City sandlots has his uniform and bat and is ready to go. He had to wait another nine years before taking over at shortstop for the New York Yankees. His name—Philip Francis Rizzuto.

Spring training, St. Petersburg, Florida, March 1930. Colonel Ruppert and his new manager, Bob Shawkey, are looking over the troops. Ruth was holding out, and the following day Jake signed his big slugger to a two-year contract at $80,000 a year.

Red Sox right-hander Charlie ("Red") Ruffing, for whom the Yankees traded early in the 1930 season.

Veteran National League catcher Eugene ("Bubbles") Hargrave, who finished up his career with the Yankees in 1930.

Outfielder Sam Byrd, called "Babe Ruth's legs" because of all the games he finished up for the aging Babe in right field. He was with the Yankees from 1929 to 1934. Sam batted .312 in 1929 and .297 in 1932 as a part-time operator. Sam left baseball at the age of thirty and became a professional golfer.

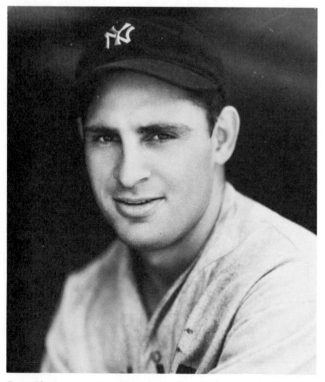

Ben Chapman, a tough, talented, and fiery outfielder who was with the Yankees from 1930 to 1936. He hit over .300 four times in New York (.316 was his high, in 1930), led the league three times in stolen bases and once in triples, and twice drove in more than 100 runs.

Spring training, 1931. Joe McCarthy, the Yankees' new manager, is sitting behind the batting cage with Ruth and Gehrig; Babe is probably holding Lou's first-base mitt. Hard-hitting outfielders with mileage on them are frequently planted at first base to save their legs—but not on this team.

Lyn Lary, Yankees utility infielder from 1929 until he was sent to the Red Sox early in 1934. Lyn was the regular shortstop in 1930 and 1931, batting .289 and .280. He lost his job to Frank Crosetti in 1932.

Chicago Cubs pitcher Charlie Root.

Joe Sewell, the man who never struck out—well, almost never. After eleven years with Cleveland (he was the man who replaced Ray Chapman after Chapman's death), the Yankees got Joe in 1931. He was their third baseman for three years, hitting .302 in '31. In his three Yankee years Joe came to bat 1,511 times and fanned on only 15 occasions. That comes to once every hundred at bats, or almost never.

The third game of the 1932 World Series against the Cubs in Wrigley Field, and an exultant Babe Ruth has just crossed home plate after hitting the most celebrated home run of his career—the one he allegedly called. He is being greeted by a smiling Lou Gehrig, who promptly belted a home run of his own. Chicago catcher Gabby Hartnett appears stunned; home-plate umpire Roy Van Graflan is unable to suppress a smile.

Frank Crosetti joined the Yankees in 1932 and remained until 1948, spending many of those years as the club's regular shortstop. Steady in the field, Frank never made much noise at the plate; his best year was 1936, when he batted .288.

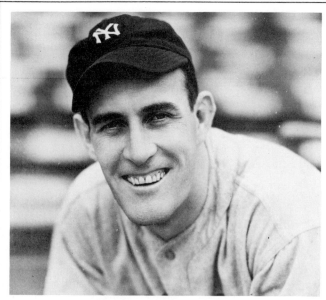

Fast-balling right-hander Johnny Allen was one of the few players McCarthy couldn't handle, though Joe tried. Johnny was hot-tempered, a heavy drinker, and alley-cat mean. He had a redeeming virtue, however—he was a winner. He was 17–4 in his rookie season of 1932 and 15–7 the next year. He fell to 5–2 in '34 and then was 13–6 in '35, after which McCarthy felt he was no longer worth the trouble, and traded him to Cleveland.

Fred ("Dixie") Walker was a prized Yankee rookie in 1933, batting .274 and hitting 15 home runs in little over half a season. A shoulder injury hampered him the next year and by 1936 he was gone. After some successful seasons with the White Sox and Tigers he ended up in Brooklyn, where he became one of the Dodgers' most popular ballplayers.

Three young men showing the joyful abandon of being young, gifted, and Yankees. Left to right; Bill Dickey, Lefty Gomez, and Lou Gehrig in 1931. Dickey hit .327 that year, Gehrig .341, and Gomez won 21. You'd be laughing too.

Bill Dickey, Yankee catcher from 1928 to 1946 (and manager for part of '46). If not the greatest catcher of all time, he was surely one of them. He was smooth behind the plate, had a strong arm, and was a shrewd handler of pitchers. And he swung one of the most potent bats in a powerful Yankee lineup. He batted over .300 eleven times, with a high of .362 in 1936. Four times he drove in more than 100 runs, peaking with 133 in 1937, a year in which he hit his career high of 29 home runs. And, like his roommate and close friend Lou Gehrig, he was durable, catching more than 100 games for thirteen consecutive seasons, a major-league record. His lifetime average is .313.

Dickey and the Cubs' Gabby Hartnett at the 1933 All-Star game. Those were the uniforms the National League players wore that year.

Judge Landis in 1933.

Ruth and Gehrig ganging up on one poor fish off Fire Island, New York, in December 1933.

Two of those sharp-eyed Yankee scouts: Paul Krichell (left) and Johnny Nee.

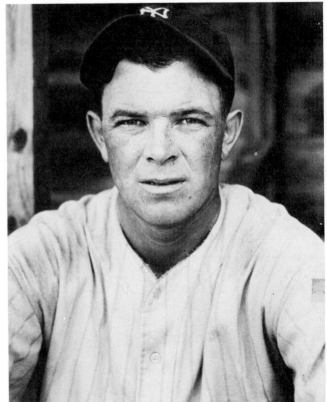

Myril Hoag, reserve outfielder for the Yankees from 1931 to 1938. An excellent utility man, Hoag batted .301 in 1936 and again in '37.

Some American League fire power at the 1933 All-Star game. Left to right: Al Simmons, Lou Gehrig, Babe Ruth, Jimmy Foxx.

Opening-day pitchers at the Stadium, 1936: Boston's Wes Ferrell and Lefty Gomez.

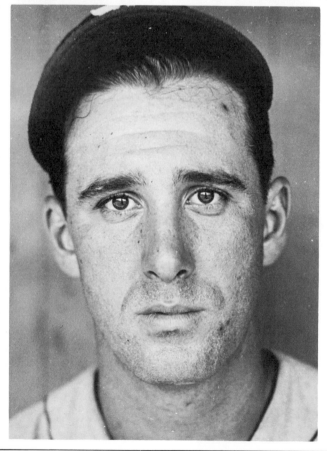

Hank Greenberg and Charlie Gehringer, stars of the Detroit Tigers' pennant-winning teams of 1934 and 1935.

Ruth in 1934, his last year as a Yankee.

February 19, 1935, at the Yankee offices in New York. Gehrig has just signed his 1935 contract and both he and Ruppert seem pleased. Lou was paid $23,000 for his Triple Crown year, 1934. The following year he asked for $35,000, was offered $27,000, and reportedly settled for $30,000. Those were the days.

George Selkirk, who had the thankless job of replacing Ruth in right field. He was with the Yankees from 1934 to 1942, batting over .300 five times and twice driving in more than 100 runs.

Johnny Broaca, a right-handed pitcher, broke in with three winning seasons—12–9 in 1934, 15–7 in '35, and 12–7 in '36. He slumped to 1–4 in 1937 and left the team shortly thereafter.

There's a new man in the National League in 1935, playing for the Boston Braves. An enormous Babe Ruth is shown here with Braves manager Bill McKechnie and Cincinnati Reds skipper Chuck Dressen. By June, Babe was gone.

Lefty Gomez, one of the Yankees' three Hall of Fame left-handers (along with Pennock and Whitey Ford). Quick with his wit and his fast ball, Gomez pitched for the Yanks from 1930 to 1942, winning 189 games and losing only 101. He won more than 20 four times, led in ERA twice, strikeouts three times, shutouts three times.

Red Ruffing in 1935. Ruffing, winner of 273 games in his big-league career, was one of the hardest-hitting pitchers of all time. He batted over .300 eight times, hitting 36 home runs, two fewer than Wes Ferrell's lifetime record for pitchers. McCarthy frequently used him as a pinch hitter.

Don Heffner, utility infielder with the Yankees from 1934 to 1937.

Red Rolfe, one of the great third basemen in Yankee history. Red, who was with the Yankees from 1934 to 1942, had his best season in 1939, when he batted .329 and led the league with 213 hits, 46 doubles, and 139 runs scored.

Pat Malone, a big, strong right-hander, who was a 20-game winner for McCarthy in Chicago. Joe got him for the Yankees in 1935 and put him in the bullpen, where Pat worked for three years. Malone's best season in New York was 1936, when he was 12–4.

Johnny Murphy, one of the greatest of Yankees relief pitchers. Johnny was with the club from 1932 to 1946. A curve-ball artist, he was 13–4 in 1937 and 12–4 in '43.

Tony Lazzeri in 1936.

Ruffing and McCarthy in 1935. No matter who else was on the staff, Ruffing was always considered the ace throughout the 1930s. "He had the stature," one of his teammates said.

Arndt Jorgens, a patient and uncomplaining man. Bill Dickey was brilliant and indestructible, but you had to have a back-up catcher just in case. The man the Yankees hired for the job was the Norwegian-born Jorgens. He was there from 1929 to 1939, averaging 70 at bats a season.

Lefty Gomez.

Jake Powell, reserve outfielder from 1936 to 1940, long enough to cash four World Series checks. Jake was an ace in the 1936 series, getting 10 hits and batting .455.

Lou Gehrig, going on and on. . . .

Irving ("Bump") Hadley, a well-traveled veteran right-hander who joined the Yankees in 1936 and remained until 1940. Bump's best was 14–4 in 1936.

The nineteen-year-old prodigy of the San Francisco Seals, Joseph Paul DiMaggio, presiding over a heaping plateful and in turn being presided over by a proud mother, 1934.

The new man in Yankee Stadium in 1936 is Joe DiMaggio, and he's in good company: Gehrig on the left, Dickey on the right. ➞

A spring training mishap delayed DiMaggio's debut until May 3, 1936. Here he is in his first game as a Yankee, swinging against Jack Knott of the St. Louis Browns at the Stadium. Joe broke in with two singles and a triple. (Note to numerologists: Joe was wearing No. 9 in those days.)

Spring training 1937 and a spectator named DiMaggio.

The 1936 season introduced two golden rookies into the American League. One was DiMaggio; the other, Cleveland's precocious seventeen-year-old, rocket-armed Bob Feller.

DiMaggio sliding safely into second base in the first inning of game two of the 1936 World Series against the Giants at the Polo Grounds. Joe was on first base when Hal Schumacher uncorked a wild pitch. Shortstop Dick Bartell has come over to cover the bag. The umpire is George Magerkurth.

Yankee rookie Tommy Henrich in 1937. His clutch hitting won him the nickname "Old Reliable" and the affection of Yankee fans. One of the most popular men ever to wear a Yankee uniform, Tommy hit .320 in his rookie year. In 1941 he hit a career-high 31 home runs. He played with the Yankees from 1937 to 1950. One of the greatest ovations in the history of Yankee Stadium was accorded Henrich in September 1942, when he came to bat for the last time before entering military service.

The front-line pitching the Giants threw at the Yankees in the 1937 World Series. Left to right: Carl Hubbell, Cliff Melton, Hal Schumacher.

Red Rolfe (left) and Johnny Murphy celebrating with soda pop after beating the Giants in the 1936 World Series.

(Left)
DiMaggio leaving the Yankee offices in February 1938. Joe was in a contract dispute with the team at the time. He finally settled for $25,000, a ten-grand increase.

Giants pitcher Hal Schumacher makes a bare-hand grab for what proved to be an errant toss from first baseman Johnny McCarthy as the Yankees' George Selkirk puts a foot on first base. George wound up on second. The umpire is Bill Stewart. The action took place in the fifth inning of game three of the 1937 World Series.

Lou Gehrig crossing the plate on his tenth and last World Series homer. It came in the ninth inning of the fourth game of the '37 series, against Carl Hubbell. Yankee batboy Tim Sullivan is greeting Lou. The catcher is Harry Danning.

Mr. and Mrs. Red Ruffing celebrating a wedding anniversary and a World Series win for Red at Leon and Eddie's, a popular New York nightspot of the time. The big day was October 7, 1937. Red had beaten the Giants 8–1 at the Stadium that afternoon.

Starting pitchers for the fifth game of the 1937 series: the Giants' Cliff Melton (left) and the Yanks' Lefty Gomez. Lefty won it and the Yankees were champs again.

McCarthy and Henrich in 1938.

A nationwide poll was taken in the summer of 1938 to determine "The Most Popular First Baseman." Here he is, Lou Gehrig, at Yankee Stadium in August with the first prize: a brand-new auto.

Meanwhile, at Ebbets Field, the Dodgers had a new first-base coach—a familiar face in an unfamiliar uniform. The Babe was hired to coach and to take extended batting practice, to draw in the fans. He did all that, but stayed for only the one year. It was the last time he drew on a uniform for pay.

Wes Ferrell, six times a 20-game winner in the American League, pitched briefly for the Yankees in 1938 and 1939. "There was no fooling around on that team," he said. "They were all business."

Cubs shortstop Billy Jurges forcing DiMaggio at second and firing on to first. The action occurred in the third game of the 1938 World Series. ➤

The Cubs' Bill Lee warming up for the fourth game of the 1938 series before a full house at Yankee Stadium. The Yanks won, completing a four-game sweep.

Cubs manager Gabby Hartnett congratulating McCarthy after the Yankee sweep in the 1938 series.

The Yankee infield in 1938. Left to right: Rolfe, Lazzeri, Gehrig, Crosetti.

Tommy Henrich in 1939.

Spring training, March 1939, at Haines City, Florida. A sharp young double-play combination up from the Yankees' Norfolk, Virginia, farm club is hoping to make the Kansas City farm club. On the left, shortstop Phil Rizzuto is taking the toss from second baseman Gerry Priddy.

Gehrig (left) and the man who replaced him at first base, Babe Dahlgren.

Rookie second baseman Joe Gordon in 1938. One of the best second basemen in Yankee history, Joe played from 1938 to 1946, when he was traded to Cleveland for Allie Reynolds. His best year was 1942, when he batted .322 and was voted the league's Most Valuable Player. His home-run high for the Yankees was 30 in 1940.

Monte Pearson pitched for the Yankees from 1936 to 1940 and had some fine seasons. He was 19–7 in 1936 and 16–7 in 1938. In World Series play he was 4–0 with a 1.01 earned-run average.

Detroit, May 2, 1939, the day Lou Gehrig took himself out of the lineup. Sitting next to the wistful Gehrig is Lefty Gomez.

Steve Sundra pitched for the Yankees from 1936 to 1940. His top year was 1939, when he was 11–1.

Gehrig and Ruth, together again at Yankee Stadium.

Lou Gehrig Appreciation Day at Yankee Stadium, July 4, 1939.

Johnny Murphy in 1939.

Joe McCarthy in 1939.

Oral Hildebrand was with the Yankees in 1939 and part of 1940, with a 10–4 season in '39.

The 1939 All-Star game was played at Yankee Stadium on July 11. Four of the participants were, left to right: Frank Crosetti, Cincinnati's Ernie Lombardi and Frank McCormick, and Red Rolfe. They got together again in that year's World Series.

Getting ready for the 1939 World Series are, left to right: Cincinnati pitcher Bucky Walters, catcher Ernie Lombardi, manager Bill McKechnie, and pitcher Paul Derringer. Walters and Derringer won 52 games between them that season, but even they couldn't prevent a four-game Yankee sweep.

Two out in the top of the ninth inning of the second game of the 1939 World Series. Cincinnati's Billy Werber is just connecting for a base hit against Monte Pearson. It was the Reds' second, and last, hit of the game, as they were shut out by Pearson 4–0.

Lou Gehrig, a dugout spectator during the 1939 series.

Cincinnati scoring a run in the second inning of game three of the 1939 World Series at old Crosley Field in Cincinnati. Billy Myers, rounding third, is coming home on Billy Werber's single. The Yankees won the game 7–3.

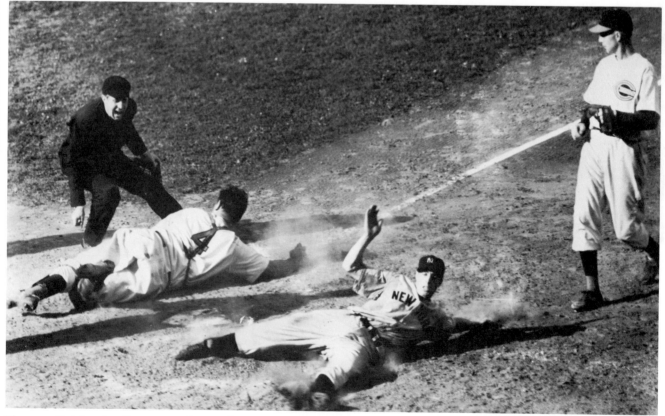

The so-called Lombardi snooze at home plate in the tenth inning of the fourth and final game of the 1939 World Series. DiMaggio is sliding home past the dazed catcher as pitcher Bucky Walters runs up. The umpire is Babe Pinelli.

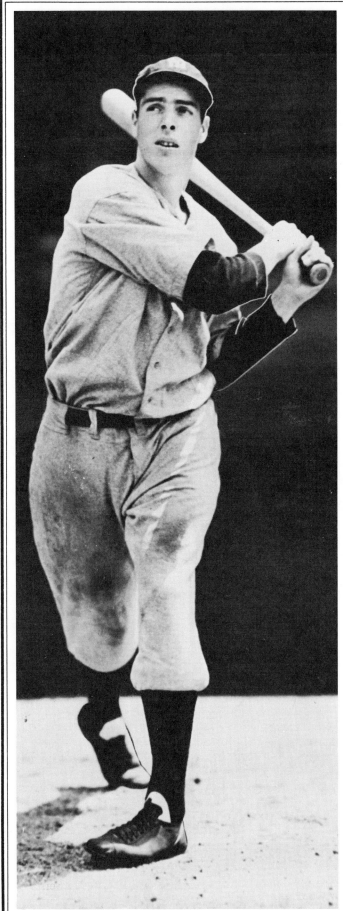

Charlie Keller, the Yankees' rookie slugger who tore up the Reds in the 1939 series. Keller was with the Yankees from 1939 to 1949 and back again briefly in 1951 and 1952. Charlie hit to all fields when he came up from Newark, but McCarthy, wanting to take advantage of the left-handed Keller's power, turned him into a pull hitter. It lowered Keller's batting average (he hit .334 in his first year with 11 home runs), but raised his home-run total. Charlie hit 33 long ones in 1941, 31 in 1943, and 30 in 1946. Three times he drove in more than 100 runs, with a peak of 122 in 1941.

Joe DiMaggio in 1939.

Stengel getting acquainted with the troops in spring training, 1949, and getting a few laughs at the same time.

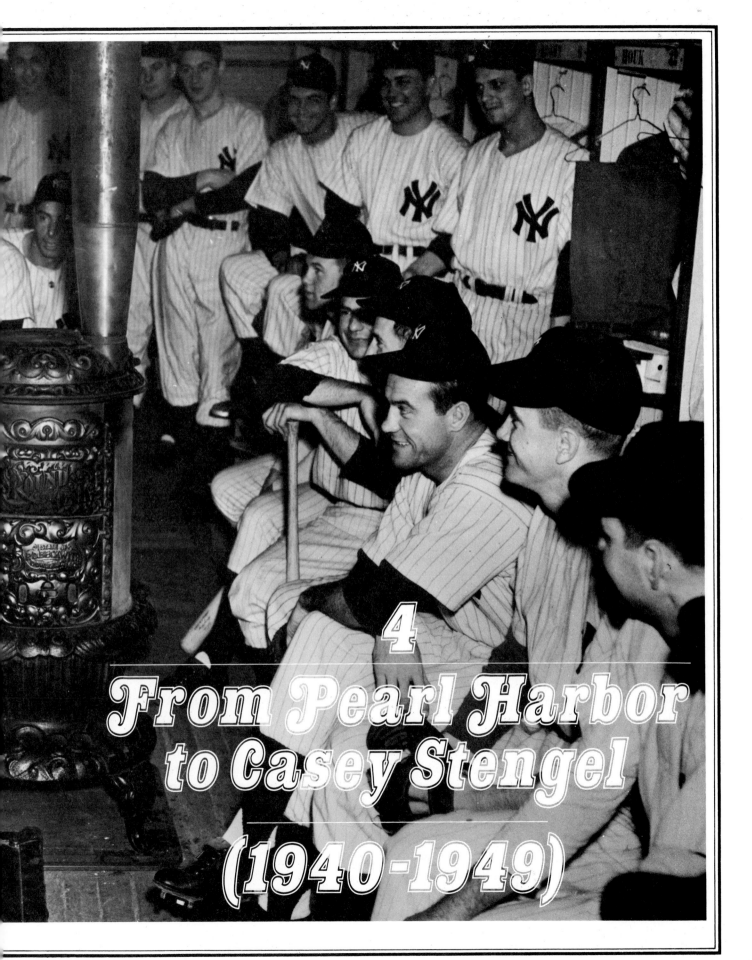

4

From Pearl Harbor to Casey Stengel

(1940-1949)

The Yankees were, in fact, planning for their old age. Their plan was simple: they would not allow it to encroach.

In the 1920s in St. Louis, Branch Rickey had begun building a farm system for the Cardinals that became unique in baseball. In those days most minor-league teams were independently owned; the teams developed their own players and then sold them to the big leagues. The shrewd, foresighted Rickey decided to circumvent this system by organizing his own network of minor-league clubs. By hiring the best scouts and signing youngsters for paltry sums, the Cardinals were able to raise their own stars. It was a self-perpetuating system (the Cardinals at one time owned the contracts of some 800 professional ballplayers), producing for the parent team such stars as Chick Hafey, Joe Medwick, Johnny Mize, the Dean brothers, and later Enos Slaughter, Terry Moore, Marty Marion, the Cooper brothers, Stan Musial, and countless others.

As far back as the early 1930s, Ed Barrow realized this was the way of the future, and in 1932 he hired a minor-league executive named George Weiss to build a farm system for the Yankees.

A frosty personality, Weiss was a clever, unsentimental, ruthlessly efficient executive. Gauging the mood and the realities of the day, he pushed ahead, wasting little time. With many minor-league franchises failing during the brutally bleak Depression years, their owners were only too glad to allow the Yankees to take over the responsibility of supplying players and assuming the club's financial obligations. Scouts were hired and sent out across the country to find and sign prospects. Representing the Yankees made the scouts' job easier, for theirs was the team with the magic name, the team of Babe Ruth and Lou Gehrig, and later, of Joe DiMaggio. They brought with them the star dust of dreams to the small towns of America.

Newark in the International League and Kansas City in the American Association were the kingpins of the system that Weiss so carefully built, the places where the last bit of spit and polish was applied to those who would wear Yankee pinstripes. The 1938 Newark Bears were the most legendary minor-league team of all time—virtually every member of the squad went to the big leagues. The Yankees, of course, could not take every one of their minor-league stars, and many were sold or shrewdly traded to other teams.

The 1940 roster was already crowded with the Yankees' homegrown product, youngsters not only taught and trained the Yankee way but also inculcated with that priceless intangible that was to become like a tenth man on the field—Yankee pride. There was a Yankee tradition, and they were part of it—as long as they produced. Because of the crowd of talented youngsters down in the minor leagues, there was very little tolerance for indifferent performance in New York, very little margin for error. Every Yankee knew there was a player almost as good, or maybe just as good, right behind him. In 1940 the Yankees had such matured farm-system players as Gordon, Keller, Henrich, reserve catcher Buddy Rosar, pitchers Chandler, Russo, Donald, Marvin Breuer, and Ernie Bonham, a burly right-hander who threw a fork ball and who soon became a star.

White Sox manager Jimmy Dykes, an irreverent sort, called McCarthy a "push-button manager," a description McCarthy detested. What Dykes meant was that whenever Joe needed a replacement all he had to do was push a button and a talented youngster would pop forth from all that Weiss and Barrow had wrought.

Nevertheless, 1940 saw the end—temporarily—of Yankee dominance. In a hard-fought three-team race with Cleveland and Detroit, they finished third, two games behind the Tigers. DiMaggio won his second batting crown with a .352 average, but Selkirk, Dickey, Crosetti, and Rolfe slumped badly. Ruffing dropped to 15 wins, and a sore arm left Gomez at the gate with a 3–3 record.

The next year, however, the Bronx Bombers made 1940 look like a mistake. They won 101 games and finished 17 ahead of Boston. Ted Williams, Boston's twenty-two-year-old third-year man with the picture-perfect swing of pure dynamite, thrilled everyone with a .406 batting average. Incredibly, Williams, who became DiMaggio's sole challenger for primacy in the sport, saw his performance overshadowed that year by his Yankee rival.

Appropriate to a game that thrives on its statistics, there are magic numbers in baseball. Not even the later achievements of Henry Aaron and Roger Maris dimmed the luster of 714 and 60, Babe Ruth's lifetime and season-high home-run numbers. And Williams's own .406 retains a special radiance. But perhaps the most immediately evocative of all baseball figures is 56. The sole owner and proprietor of that number is Joe DiMaggio.

It began innocuously enough, on May 15, 1941, at Yankee Stadium, with a first-inning single against Chicago White Sox left-hander Edgar Smith. Joe went one for four that day. Not until the night of

July 17 at Cleveland did a Yankee game pass without a hit by DiMaggio.

There is something lonely and heroic about an extended batting streak. It is one man alone against the world, with the odds and the pressure bearing down ever more heavily each day. For DiMaggio the hitting streak was a perfect showcase. By now he stood alone, separated from other players by the incomparable power and grace of his talents. The streak served only to individualize him further, raise him to an even loftier, more rarefied plateau. And no ballplayer was ever more comfortable under pressure. If he felt it, it did not show. Pride overcame all.

The 56-game hitting streak was DiMaggio and baseball at their best. It caught the imagination of the entire country in that last prewar summer. Only baseball, with its day-in, day-out schedule, could put on this kind of show, and having its mightiest star at stage center made it all the more exciting, made it right.

The first record to fall under his remorseless forward flow was the Yankee team hitting streak of twenty-nine, shared by Roger Peckinpaugh (then managing Cleveland) and Joe's fine predecessor at center field, Earle Combs (coaching for the Red Sox that year and watching Williams battle on toward .400). On June 17 Joe set a new Yankee record by hitting in his thirtieth straight game, his lone hit being a bad-hop single off the shoulder of White Sox shortstop Luke Appling. The American League record of forty-one games set by George Sisler in 1922 was the next target; in a double-header in Washington on July 1, Joe tied and broke Sisler's mark. A few days later DiMaggio's home run broke the major-league record of forty-four games set by Wee Willie Keeler of the Baltimore Orioles (then in the National League) in 1897.

Now it was a matter of how far he could go. The pressure was on everyone—on opposing pitchers, who both wanted to stop him as well as give him a fair chance at bat; on official scorers, dreading having to make a questionable decision; and on McCarthy, who on several occasions had to forgo strategy and let Joe swing at 3–0 pitches when the streak was on the line ("I wasn't taking such a bad risk," the whimsical McCarthy said later).

Establishing a new record caused no letdown in DiMaggio's performance. In fact he got even hotter as the streak rolled on. Through the next eleven games his hitting became torrid—twenty-four hits in forty-four official times at bat for a .545 average.

On the night of July 17 more than 65,000 fans crowded Cleveland's cavernous Municipal Stadium to watch Joe reach for number 57. He came to bat in the first inning against left-hander Al Smith. Third baseman Ken Keltner, one of the finest gloves in the league, was playing back near the outfield grass, as if daring Joe to bunt. (DiMaggio had not bunted once during the streak. When asked if his perfect player could, indeed, bunt, McCarthy replied, "I don't know, nor do I ever have any intention of finding out.")

DiMaggio hit a hard grounder; Keltner made a fine play and threw him out. In the fourth Joe walked. In the seventh he hit another sharp ground ball to Keltner and was again thrown out. In the eighth, facing right-hander Jim Bagby, DiMaggio hit the ball well but right at shortstop Lou Boudreau, who took it and started a double play. It was Joe's last time at bat. The streak was over.

McCarthy saw the owner of the Indians after the game and the man was jubilant, congratulating everyone in sight for having stopped the streak. "But the next day," McCarthy said, "when he saw the ball park less than half full, he wasn't so happy."

With DiMaggio's hitting streak over, the Yankees went about with the season's primary business, winning the pennant, which they did with ease. They were 25–4 in July for an American League record of .862 for one month. They clinched the pennant on September 4, the earliest date in big-league history.

There was a notable addition to the Yankee lineup that year. From the Kansas City farm club came an agile, quick-handed, 5′6″ New York City native, Phil Rizzuto. Rizzuto, who became the greatest Yankee shortstop, replaced Crosetti and batted .307 in his rookie year. The Henrich–Keller–DiMaggio outfield, one of the Yankees' all-time best, averaged 30 home runs and 100 runs batted in.

It was another all-New York World Series that year, but this time the Yankees' rivals were the Brooklyn Dodgers. The Dodgers, managed by ex-Yankee Leo Durocher, were a noisy, brawling, highly talented club that had brought Brooklyn its first pennant in twenty-one years.

The series was hotly contested and tightly played, with pitching dominating. It would have been a rather unmemorable October joust except for what occurred in game four. The first two games had been 3–2 scores, Ruffing winning the opener for the Yankees, Whitlow Wyatt the second game for the Dodgers. The third game was a sharp pitching duel between Brooklyn's veteran knuckle baller Fred Fitzsimmons and the Yankees' Marius Russo. In the seventh inning of a scoreless game Russo lined a ball off of Fitzsimmons's knee and the Dodger pitcher had to leave the game. The Yankees scored two runs off his successor, Hugh Casey, and went on to win 2–1.

The following afternoon at Ebbets Field the Dodgers seemed to have deadlocked the series with a 4–3 win; *seemed* is precisely the word, and it only seemed that way for a split second. With Brooklyn ahead 4–3, and two out and nobody on base for the Yankees in the top of the ninth, Hugh Casey struck out Tommy Henrich for the third out. Or so it seemed. The pitch that Casey threw was an explosive, unhittable curve (the break on the ball was so sharp that some people insisted it had to have been a spitter); unhittable, and, in this instance, uncatchable, too. Dodger catcher Mickey Owen could not handle the ball and it rolled away, a dropped third strike, enabling the ever-alert and hustling Henrich to reach first base. What happened after that was awesome.

"When people talk about that top of the ninth inning," Henrich said years later, "all they seem to remember is Hugh Casey, Mickey Owen, and me. I always say, 'Wait a minute. You're forgetting a few guys. What about DiMaggio coming up and hitting a screaming line drive to left for a single? And then what about Keller coming up and doubling off of that right-field screen to score us? And then Dickey walking, and Joe Gordon doubling to left for two more."

That was exactly what happened. The drama of the dropped ball has overshadowed what remains one of the most stunning rallies in series history. The following day Bonham beat a demoralized Dodger team and the Yankees were again world champions.

The country was at war by the time the next season rolled around. Stars like Hank Greenberg and Bob Feller were already in the service and many others soon followed. But outside of the late-season departure of Tommy Henrich to the coast guard and first baseman Johnny Sturm to the army, the Yankee roster remained relatively intact. An acquisition from the National League, Buddy Hassett, took over at first base and gave the New Yorkers a fine year before joining the navy after the season.

After a bitter contract dispute with Barrow, DiMaggio (who finally signed for around $43,000) had an off year, batting .305 but driving in 114 runs. Joe Gordon, however, put together a season that won him the Most Valuable Player Award, the third Yankee, after Gehrig in '36 and DiMaggio in '39 and '41, to be so named. Gordon batted .322, drove in

103 runs and performed with acrobatic brilliance in the field. Bonham was the ace that year with a 21–5 record, followed by Chandler's 16–5 mark and a 15–4 season by another graduate of the farm system, right-hander Hank Borowy. Ruffing, at the age of thirty-eight, racked up a 14–7 record. The Yankees won 103 games and finished ahead of the Red Sox by nine.

The New Yorkers were perhaps overconfident when they took the field for the 1942 World Series against the St. Louis Cardinals. But the Cardinals, virtually all of them products of the St. Louis farm system, were a young (the team's average age was twenty-six), hungry, perpetually hustling club. They had won a grueling pennant race against the Dodgers, winning 106 games to Brooklyn's 104. Their top hitters were Enos Slaughter and rookie Stan Musial, their aces 20-game winners Mort Cooper and Johnny Beazley.

In one of the most stunning October upsets ever, the Cardinals swept the Yankees in four straight after bowing to Ruffing in the opener. Though they were outhit, the Cards got two route-going jobs from Beazley and another strong game from lefty Ernie White, spelling the difference.

By the time the 1943 season began the Yankees, like most other big-league clubs, had seen their roster depleted by departures to military service. DiMaggio, Rizzuto, Hassett, Henrich, and Ruffing were gone. The Yankees obtained first baseman Nick Etten from the Phillies and dug into their farm system for other replacements. From Newark came third baseman Billy Johnson. Another Newark product, Johnny Lindell, who throughout his minor-league career had been a hard-hitting pitcher, was converted to an outfielder. Also from Newark came outfielder Bud Metheny and utility infielder George ("Snuffy") Stirnweiss, who filled in at shortstop along with the veteran Crosetti. The thirty-six-year-old Dickey, playing his last year before joining the navy, batted .351 to lead the team (Bill got into only 85 games that year).

Chandler, the Yankees' third straight MVP, posted a 20–4 record, enhancing it with the league's lowest earned-run average since 1919, 1.64. Bonham won 15 and Borowy 14 as the team finished 13½ games ahead of Washington. Murphy was 12–4 coming out of the bullpen.

It was another Yankee-Cardinal series. This time the Yankees won it in six games. A two-run homer by Dickey in game six gave Chandler a 2–0 win and the Yankees the championship.

By 1944 the roster had been all but picked clean of

regulars by the armed forces. Gordon, Dickey, Keller, Johnson, and Chandler went off to war, and the best McCarthy could do with his patchwork lineup was third place. The only bright spots were Etten's league-leading 22 home runs and a strong .319 season by Stirnweiss, installed at second in place of Gordon. Snuffy led the league in runs, hits, triples, and stolen bases. Borowy's 17 wins headed the staff.

The Yankees marked time again in 1945, finishing fourth but only 6½ games behind the pennant-winning Tigers. Again Stirnweiss lit up an otherwise dreary season for the team, winning the batting championship on the final day with a modest .309 average.

Playing as regulars in the Yankee lineup in those years were men named Mike Milosevich, Oscar Grimes, Hersh Martin, Don Savage, Russ Derry, Mike Garbark. There was, after all, a war on.

At about this time the Yankees were sold by the Ruppert heirs for $2.8 million to a triumvirate of new owners: Dan Topping, Del Webb, and Larry MacPhail. Topping was a millionaire who was often characterized in the newspapers as a "playboy" or "sportsman." Webb had made his money in construction. MacPahil was well known in the baseball world; a man of tempestuous and unpredictable behavior, he was one of the game's brilliant innovators. While running the Cincinnati Reds in the mid-1930s he had forcefed night baseball on his skeptical colleagues. Taking over a moribund Brooklyn franchise a few years later, he installed lights in Ebbets Field, spent large sums of money and built the Dodgers into a winner, after which he rushed off to help win the war with a lieutenant colonel's commission. MacPhail and his partners brought night ball to Yankee Stadium in 1946.

The familiar faces reassembled at St. Petersburg in the spring of 1946. Etten was held over at first base, Gordon and Rizzuto were back at second and short, while third was manned by Stirnweiss and Johnson. The Henrich–Keller–DiMaggio combine was reunited in the outfield, while the bulk of the catching was handled by a left-handed-hitting receiver with power, Aaron Robinson.

The magic wasn't quite there yet, however, as the Yankees ran a poor third behind a power-hitting Red Sox team, finishing an unaccustomed 17 games behind. But financially the season was a success for the Yankees; the fans turned out in droves to see their returning favorites, working the turnstiles for a record 2,265,512 admissions. This shattered the club's own previous high by more than a million, an astonishing mark considering the Yankees were never really in the race that year.

DiMaggio dipped under .300 for the first time, batting .295, which nonetheless led the team; it was the first time since 1917 that the Yankees were without a .300 bat in their lineup. Gordon had a woeful .210 season, while Rizzuto and Henrich showed some rust on their bats. Chandler returned with a 20–8 season and righty Bill Bevens was 16–13.

For the first time in fifteen years the Yankees underwent a managerial change. McCarthy, increasingly uncomfortable with the new ownership—in particular with MacPhail's second-guessing—resigned on May 24, retiring to his farm outside of Buffalo. (Joe returned in 1948 to manage the Red Sox for several seasons.) The new manager was Bill Dickey. Popular and knowledgeable, the veteran catcher, now thirty-nine and at the end of his playing career, seemed a good choice. But by September Bill had become disenchanted with managing and resigned. Coach Johnny Neun ran the club during the final weeks of the season.

It had been an awkward and disappointing year for the great team from the Bronx, but some new people had arrived who would soon make a difference. One was a big, strong right-hander from the Pacific Coast League, Vic Raschi. Another was a squat, homely, unlikely-looking ballplayer up from Newark named Lawrence Peter ("Yogi") Berra, who in time became not only one of the purest and most lethal swings in baseball, but one of the all-time Yankee greats. At first awkward, shy, dropping priceless malapropisms, Berra soon grew into not only a dangerous power hitter but also a superb defensive catcher and shrewd handler of pitchers. A kindly and modest man, blessed with one of the most priceless nicknames in all sports, Berra was and remains one of the most beloved of all Yankees. He arrived at the tail end of the '46 season, played in seven games, batted .364 and hit two home runs. A pronounced pull hitter, his swing was designed for the Stadium's short porch in right field.

The Yankees made two significant postseason moves. Dissatisfied with Etten, they signed free agent George McQuinn. The thirty-seven-year-old McQuinn had been in the Yankee farm system in the 1930s but had been blocked at the top by Gehrig. He later had a productive career with the St. Louis Browns, put in a mediocre year with the Athletics in 1946 and had been released, considered to be washed up.

The other Yankee move was of greater significance, paying long-term dividends: second baseman

Joe Gordon was traded to Cleveland for right-hander Allie Reynolds, a husky fireballer who prospered mightily in New York. Because of his Creek Indian heritage, Reynolds fell heir to baseball's hoary "Chief" nickname. In time, though, Allie's sterling mound work got him promoted to "Superchief."

The Yankees hired one of the game's veteran managers to lead the team in 1947—Stanley ("Bucky") Harris. A one-time boy wonder who had won two pennants as player-manager for Washington in 1924 and 1925, Harris had since led Detroit, the Boston Red Sox, Washington again, and the Philadelphia Phillies, all with little success. He was a sound baseball man though, low-keyed and easygoing. Led by Harris, the Yankees rose to the top once more in 1947, winning the pennant handily, 12 games ahead of second-place Detroit.

McQuinn coaxed an excellent .304 season out of his aging body, while Rizzuto, Johnson, and Henrich all came back with strong showings. DiMaggio batted .315 and was voted MVP for the third time. Aaron Robinson caught most of the games, but young Berra was breaking in. ("Bill Dickey is learning me his experience," Yogi said, and the writers began leaning closer when the new man spoke, intrigued by his uniquely phrased wisdom. In time Yogi would be paid the high accolade of having many fractured quotes attributed to him, some of them manufactured out of whole cloth.) Keller, his career destroyed by a bad back, was replaced in the outfield by Lindell.

Reynolds led the staff with 19 wins, followed by rookie Frank Shea's 14–5 record. But the big story on the Yankees that year was a hitherto erratic fast-balling lefty named Joe Page. Page, a big, handsome, fast-living bon vivant, had had middling success as a starter for several years when Harris turned him into a relief specialist (with the departure of Murphy the year before, the Yankees were without a bullpen ace). Page relieved 54 times that season, winning 14 games and saving 17 others, thus having a hand in nearly a third of the team's 97 victories.

The World Series reunited the Yankees and Dodgers. It proved to be one of the most exciting series ever, the Yankees winning in seven. There were two standout moments. The first occurred in game four, at Ebbets Field. Bill Bevens, the Yankee pitcher, had a no-hitter going into the ninth inning—an untidy no-hitter to be sure, walking eight men as he nursed along a 2–1 lead. Bevens was a big right-hander who had joined the Yankees during the war years and stayed on; his best year was 1946, with a 16–13 record. He slumped to 7–13 in '47 and

was starting only because Harris had seen his staff chewed up by Dodger bats in game three.

A no-hitter never having been pitched in World Series play, the tension gripping Ebbets field was palpable as the Dodgers came to bat in the bottom of the ninth inning. Having suffered an unassisted triple play at the hands of Bill Wambsganss in the 1920 series and Mickey Owen's dropped third strike in the 1941 show, Brooklyn fans were no doubt sitting in fear of having to endure the ultimate humiliation. (Even if they had, it still wouldn't have been the darkest moment in Dodger history; after all, on the road ahead waited Bobby Thomson, Don Larsen, and, finally, a lawyer named Walter O'Malley.) Bruce Edwards, the first batter, flied deep to DiMaggio in center; one out. Carl Furillo drew Bevens's ninth walk. Johnny Jorgensen fouled to McQuinn for out number two.

Then, as baseball announcers like to observe, "the wheels began to turn" as Brooklyn manager Burt Shotton started playing a hand that got hotter and hotter. He sent utility outfielder Al Gionfriddo in to run for Furillo and Pete Reiser up to bat for the pitcher, Hugh Casey. Reiser, a potent hitter, had been sidelined with a broken bone in his ankle, but such was Shotton's faith in this great player that Burt did not hesitate to employ him in this situation. A moment later Harris was to show similar respect; Gionfriddo lit out for second and stole the bag, coming in under a somewhat high throw from Berra. Harris then made a critical and unorthodox move—he ordered Reiser, the potential winning run, put on first base, a move which sent a shudder through baseball purists, who insist you never put the winning run on. Reiser, unable to run, was replaced at first by Eddie Miksis.

Shotton, his managerial I.Q. now at genius level, sent veteran infielder Harry ("Cookie") Lavagetto up to bat for Eddie Stanky, a move not every manager might have made; Stanky was a pesky contact hitter and had been hit for only twice in 146 games that season. Lavagetto, in the waning days of a fine if unspectacular career, crowned that career with one of baseball's historic bashes: he drove a Bevens pitch on a line to right field. The ball struck low on the right-field wall, Henrich had a moment's worth of trouble picking it up, and the two Dodger pinch runners sped across the plate. It was a heartbreaking moment for Bevens as jubilation ripped through the borough of Brooklyn, a place never known for sedate deportment.

Unfazed, the Yankees came back the next afternoon as Frank Shea won his second game of the series, nipping the Dodgers 2–1. The game ended on a note of high drama: with a Dodger on second and two out, Lavagetto pinch-hit once more. Could Cookie do it again? That's just what Tommy Henrich in right field was wondering. "I was standing near DiMaggio in the outfield," Henrich recalled, "and we look at each other. Would you believe that he said to me, 'For Christ's sake, say a prayer'? That's exactly what he said. DiMaggio. Shea strikes Lavagetto out. We run into the clubhouse and I go over to Crosetti. 'Get a load of this,' I said. 'What do you think the big guy said when Lavagetto came up?' And I tell him. Crosetti's reaction is, 'Why didn't you tell *him* to pray?' That's pretty good, right? So I go over to DiMaggio and repeat it. And Joe says, 'I *was* praying. I wasn't sure if I was getting through.'"

The two clubs slugged it out in the sixth game at Yankee Stadium, the Dodgers coming up on top with an 8–6 win. In a series dominated by the irregulars, Al Gionfriddo emerged as the hero in this game. In the bottom of the sixth, Brooklyn leading 8–5, the Yankees had men on first and second and DiMaggio at bat. Joe tied into one and drove it out toward the visitors' bullpen in left field, 415 feet away. Gionfriddo went back at top speed, reached up and took it, depriving DiMaggio of a probable game-tying home run. Baseball historians have noted that the catch evoked DiMaggio's only display of emotion on a ball field. As he rounded second base and saw that the ball had been caught, Joe stopped and aimed a frustrated little kick at the ground.

The next day, with Page relieving in the fifth inning and firing five innings of one-hit ball, the Yankees wrapped it up, 5–2.

Only Larry MacPhail could bring a topper to a World Series victory. During the postgame celebration in the Yankee clubhouse, MacPhail announced he was selling his one-third interest in the club to Topping and Webb, who were relieved to be rid of their brilliant but erratic partner. MacPhail retired

from the game to his Maryland farm, leaving behind a career of innovation, controversy, brawls, and glory that has few parallels in baseball history.

The next year, 1948, produced a rarity in Yankee annals—the team was nosed out in a close pennant race. It was a three-team contest between New York, Boston, and Cleveland. The Yankees were eliminated on the next-to-the-last day. The Indians went on to beat Boston (managed by Joe McCarthy) in a one-game play-off.

It was a big year for DiMaggio: a .320 average, 39 home runs, 155 runs batted in. Lindell batted .317, Henrich .308, and Berra, splitting his time behind the plate and in the outfield, .305. But Rizzuto and Stirnweiss had subpar years, and McQuinn, who slumped to .248, was released after the season.

On the mound, Page had been unable to repeat his superb 1947 season, but the Yankee starting rotation contained what became a familiar litany of doom and defeat for the rest of the league—Raschi, Reynolds, and Lopat. The Yankees had engineered another splendid transaction in obtaining the crafty left-hander Eddie Lopat from the White Sox in exchange for Aaron Robinson and several minor leaguers. Again the remarkable Yankee depth in talent—they knew Berra was ready to assume the job—enabled them to trade their front-line catcher for a needed starter.

The Big Three were winners; Raschi was 19–8, Lopat 17–11, Reynolds 16–7. Shea, suffering with arm miseries, slumped to 9–10 and ceased being a factor in Yankee pitching plans.

After MacPhail's departure, the job of general manager was handed to Weiss, with Ed Barrow retiring. The new GM's first move came the day after the World Series. At a news conference called at the 21 Club, the Yankees announced that they had hired a new manager. Having once played in the outfield for the Dodgers and the Giants, the new man was now completing the New York baseball circuit. His name: Casey Stengel.

Hard-throwing right-hander Atley Donald joined the Yankees in 1938 and pitched for them until 1945. He had two particularly strong years: 1939, when he was 13–3, and 1942, when he was 11–3. Donald wasn't through performing services for the Yankees though, even after hanging up his spikes. Scouting in Louisiana for the club, he signed up Ron Guidry.

Right-hander Marvin Breuer pitched for the Yankees from 1939 to 1943. His best year was 1941, when he was 9–7.

Joe McCarthy and Ed Barrow in 1940.

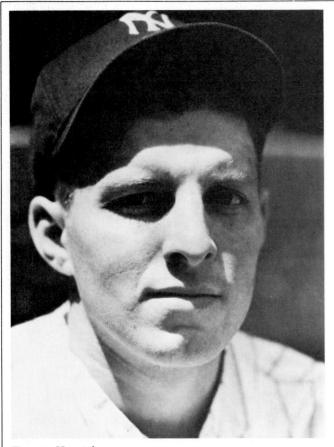

Tommy Henrich.

Johnny Sturm, Yankees first baseman in 1941. Johnny only played that one year, batted .239, then went into the service and did not return to baseball.

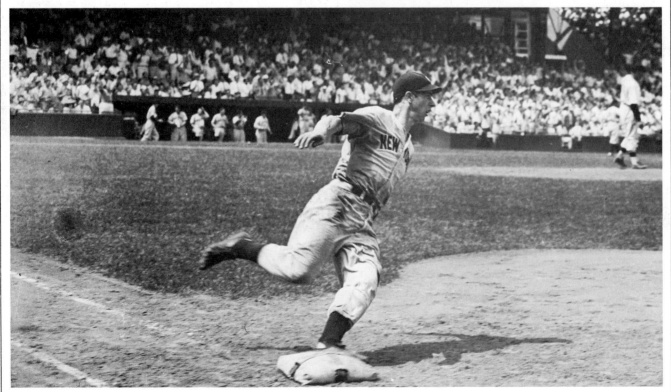

June 30, 1941; the Yankees are playing a double-header against the Washington Senators, and DiMaggio has hit safely in both games, breaking George Sisler's American League record by hitting in forty-two consecutive games.

Cleveland's third baseman Ken Keltner, whose fine defensive play helped stop DiMaggio's hitting streak.

The DiMaggio cut.

Ted Williams, whose dramatic ninth-inning home run has just won the 1941 All-Star game, being congratulated by DiMaggio in the clubhouse.

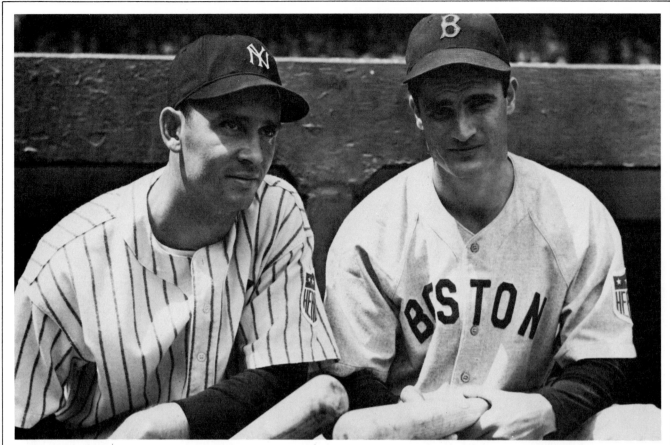

The American League's two top second basemen, the Yankees' Joe Gordon and Boston's Bobby Doerr, in 1941.

Marius Russo, a left-hander with the Yankees from 1939 to 1946. His best year was 1940, when he was 14–8.

Warren ("Buddy") Rosar, Yankee catcher from 1939 to 1942. Buddy backed up Bill Dickey and did a good job. He batted .298 in 73 games in 1940, his best and busiest year as a Yankee. He was traded to Cleveland in 1943.

Rival managers at the opening of the 1941 World Series at Yankee Stadium: the Yankees' Joe McCarthy on the left, Brooklyn's Leo Durocher on the right.

Brooklyn's Hugh Casey, who threw the fatal pitch to Tommy Henrich.

Mickey Owen, the man who missed the third strike.

Henrich has swung and missed, umpire Larry Goetz has called him out, but the ball is rolling, rolling.

These smiling Yankees are the men who snatched victory from defeat. Shown here in the Yankee clubhouse moments after beating Brooklyn in game four of the 1941 World Series are, left to right: Tommy Henrich, the only man to start a triumphant World Series rally by striking out; Joe DiMaggio, who singled; Charlie Keller, who doubled in the winning runs; and Joe Gordon, who doubled in two more just for luck.

Joe DiMaggio in 1942.

John ("Buddy") Hassett, a sharp-hitting first baseman the Yankees acquired from the Boston Braves in 1942. Buddy batted .284 and then went off to the navy. He did not return to the big leagues after the war.

Phil Rizzuto in 1942.

Ernie ("Tiny") Bonham, one of McCarthy's aces in the early 1940s. The burly right-hander, who featured a fork ball, joined the Yankees in 1940 and broke in with a 9–3 record and 1.90 earned-run average. Ernie's big year was 1942, when he was 21–5, leading the league in winning percentage (.808), complete games (22), and shutouts (6). He was with the Yankees through the 1946 season.

Hank Borowy, another right-handed winner out of the farm system. Hank joined the Yankees in 1942 and had records of 15–4, 14–9, 17–12, and 10–5 when he was waived out of the league and sold to the Chicago Cubs in 1945 for $100,000, a deal that never really made sense for the Yankees. It was rumored that Larry MacPhail, by that time running the club, owed a favor to the Cub management. Borowy was 11–2 for the Cubs, helping them win the 1945 pennant.

Starting pitchers for game three of the 1942 World Series at the Stadium: St. Louis Cardinals left-hander Ernie White (left) and the Yankees' Spud Chandler. White shut the New Yorkers out, 2–0 in a brilliant pitching duel, with Chandler allowing just three hits and one run in eight innings. Spud joined the Yankees in 1937 and pitched for them until 1947. He was 20–4 in 1943 and 20–8 in 1946, leading in earned-run average in '43 and again in '47. Chandler was extremely difficult to beat; his lifetime winning percentage is .717, the highest in major-league history among pitchers with 100 or more wins. His lifetime record is 109–43.

A group of triumphant St. Louis Cardinals celebrating their second-game victory over the Yankees in the 1942 series. Front, manager Billy Southworth (left) and catcher Walker Cooper. Rear, left to right: outfielder Enos Slaughter, outfielder Stan Musial, winning pitcher Johnny Beazley, and third baseman Whitey Kurowski.

First baseman Nick Etten, whom the Yankees acquired from the Philadelphia Phillies to replace the departed Buddy Hassett in 1943. Nick gave a pallid Yankee lineup some punch during the war years, leading the league with 22 home runs in 1944 and with 111 runs batted in in 1945. He remained with the club through the 1946 season.

Joe Gordon, the American League's Most Valuable Player in 1942.

Rollie Hemsley; the Yankees acquired this fine veteran receiver in 1942 and he remained with them until 1944, catching 81 games that year and batting .268. Rollie drank a bit, but as former teammate Bob Feller said, "Rollie could catch drunk better than most guys could sober."

Charlie Keller in 1943.

The 1943 Yankee infield. Left to right: second baseman Joe Gordon, first baseman Nick Etten, shortstop George Stirnweiss, third baseman Billy Johnson.

(Above)
Arthur ("Bud") Metheny, outfielder with the Yankees from 1943 to 1946. A regular during the war years, the best Bud could do was .261 in 1943.

(Left)
Billy Johnson, Yankee third baseman from 1943 to 1951. Billy was a tough, hard-nosed ballplayer. Twice he drove in more than 90 runs and in 1948 batted .294, his career high.

A controversial call in the sixth inning of the opening game of the 1943 World Series at Yankee Stadium. Frank Crosetti has not touched the bag yet, while Cardinal first baseman Ray Sanders has the ball—or seems to. Umpire Beans Reardon called Crosetti safe, igniting a heated argument. The play was crucial, as it led to a two-run inning for the Yanks, who won the game 4–2.

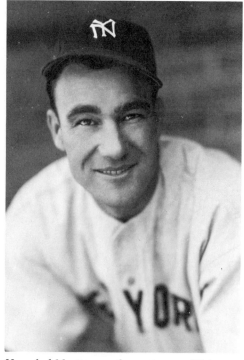

George ("Snuffy") Stirnweiss, an infielder who was the star of the Yankees' wartime teams. He batted .319 in 1944 and a league-leading .309 in 1945, topping the league in hits, triples, runs scored, and stolen bases in each of those years. After the war Stirnweiss dropped to a .250 hitter. He was with the Yankees from 1943 to 1950.

Herschel Martin, another veteran addition to the Yankees' patchwork lineup during the war. He was with the team in 1944 and 1945, batting .302 in '44.

Originally a pitcher in the Yankee farm system, Johnny Lindell made it to the big club as an outfielder, playing from 1941 to 1950. He hit .300 in 1944 and .317 in 1948. He led the league in triples in 1943 and 1944.

Charles ("Butch") Wensloff spent one full year with the Yankees—1943—had a 13–11 record with a 2.54 earned-run average and then went into voluntary retirement. He was back to pitch briefly in 1947.

Big right-hander Allen Gettel pitched creditably for the Yankees in 1945 and 1946, winning 15 and losing 15 overall. He was traded to Cleveland in 1947.

Walter ("Monk") Dubiel was a regular starter for the Yankees during the years 1944–1945. The big right-hander had records of 13–13 and 10–9.

Del Webb.

Larry MacPhail, one of the Yankees' new owners (still in uniform), conferring with George Weiss (center) and Ed Barrow in New York in January 1945.

Dan Topping.

Phil Rizzuto (left) and George Stirnweiss practicing the double play in spring training, 1946.

Mel Allen, for many years the "Voice of the Yankees" and one of the most popular of all baseball announcers.

Joe DiMaggio in 1946, back from the wars.

Bob Feller, who no-hit the Yankees on April 30, 1946, at the Stadium, winning 1–0.

The great outfield reunited after the war. Left to right: Charlie Keller, Joe DiMaggio, and Tommy Henrich, in spring training, St. Petersburg, Florida, March 1946.

DiMaggio, McCarthy, and MacPhail in the spring of 1946. Once MacPhail took over the team, McCarthy's days were numbered.

Randy Gumpert, a right-hander who pitched for the Yankees from 1946 to 1948, when he was waived to the White Sox. Gumpert had one very effective year for the Yankees, 1946, when he was 11–3 with a 2.31 earned-run average.

Aaron Robinson was with the Yankees from 1943 to 1947. Catching most of the games in 1946, the left-handed-hitting Robinson batted .297 with 16 home runs. With the arrival of Yogi Berra, however, he became expendable, and in 1948 was traded to the White Sox as part of the deal for Eddie Lopat.

Some of the Boston firepower that drove the Red Sox to the pennant in 1946. Left to right: Ted Williams, Johnny Pesky, Dominic DiMaggio.

August 26, 1946, at Yankee Stadium. DiMaggio slides home safely as Detroit's catcher Paul Richards applies the tag a moment too late. The umpire is Bill Summers. The interested spectator in pinstripes is Joe Gordon.

April 27, 1947: Babe Ruth Day at the Stadium. The Babe, already showing the ravages of the cancer that was to take his life sixteen months later, is addressing the crowd. Included in the semicircle around Ruth are, left to right: National League President Ford Frick, Yankees announcer Mel Allen, New York's Francis Cardinal Spellman, and baseball commissioner Happy Chandler. The two men on the right are not identified.

Yogi Berra in 1947, his first full year as a Yankee.

George McQuinn in 1947.

Phil Rizzuto.

Manager Bucky Harris standing between two of his pitchers, young right-hander Vic Raschi (left) and veteran right-hander Bobo Newsom. Bobo was picked up from Washington in midseason in 1947, went 7–5, and was released after the season.

Frank ("Spec") Shea, a highly talented pitcher who saw his major-league career aborted by arm problems. Shea was with the Yankees from 1947 to 1951, with a particularly effective rookie season, when he was 14–5, and added two more wins against the Dodgers in the World Series.

Allie Reynolds, who came to the Yankees from Cleveland in 1947 in a trade for Joe Gordon. One of the hardest throwers of his time, Reynolds pitched winning ball for the Yankees from 1947 to 1954, when a back injury forced his retirement. He was 19–8 in 1947. His finest year with the Yankees was 1952, when he was 20–8, with a league-leading 2.06 earned-run average and a top strikeout total of 160. Stengel used him both as a starter and reliever in Allie's last two years; coming out of that bullpen with his fast ball, Reynolds was awesome.

Sherman Lollar, another first-rate catcher roadblocked in New York by Berra. He saw a minimal amount of action with the Yankees in 1947 and 1948 before being traded. He remained in the American League for another fifteen years, having a fine career with the Browns and White Sox.

Bobby Brown, Yankee third baseman with a sharp bat. Bobby was with the Yankees from 1946 to 1954, batting .300 in '47 and '48. Brown was especially tough under World Series pressure, batting .439 in four series. Brown retired in 1954 to pursue a career in medicine and became a practicing physician in Texas.

Joe Page in 1947, making one of his trademark departures from the Yankee bullpen. Joe was with the Yankees from 1944 to 1950, the first three years as a moderately successful starter. Moved to the bullpen by Harris in 1947, however, he became a star. His great years were '47, when he was 14–8 with 17 saves, and '49, when he was 13–8 with 27 saves.

The first game of the 1947 World Series, Yankees vs. Dodgers, and this is part of the huge crowd—over 73,000—on hand to watch the Yanks win it, 5–3.

It's just happened—Lavagetto's historic line drive is heading for the right-field wall and Miksis, the Dodger base runner, is on his way.

A disappointed Bill Bevens manages a brave smile in greeting Lavagetto the next day.

The Gionfriddo catch in game six of the 1947 Series. Joe D. thought it was gone.

In spite of all the Dodger heroics, the Yankees won the series. Celebrating after their victory in game seven are Joe Page (who won it with five innings of one-hit relief pitching), manager Bucky Harris, and Joe DiMaggio.

Yogi Berra (right) and Yankee coach Chuck Dressen strolling down the street in St. Petersburg, Florida, in March 1948. Dressen, who coached for the Yankees in 1947 and 1948, later became skipper of the Brooklyn Dodgers and other big-league teams.

Bob Lemon in 1948, a 20-game winner for Cleveland and future pennant-winning manager of the Yankees.

Clarence ("Cuddles") Marshall, a right-hander who was with the Yankees for parts of three seasons from 1946 to 1949.

Bob Porterfield in 1948, just before leaving the Newark Bears to join the Yankees. Bob, a hard-throwing right-hander, was considered the choice of the Yankee farm system at the time, but arm problems prevented him from fulfilling his promise in New York. He was with the Yankees until 1951, when he was traded to Washington, for whom he later became a 20-game winner. The best he ever did for the Yankees was 5–3 in 1948.

Eddie Lopat, just before being traded by the White Sox to the Yankees. Eddie pitched for the Yankees from 1948 to 1955 and was 109–51 for them. His best year was 21–9 in 1951. In 1953 he was the league's most effective pitcher, with a 16–4 record, league-leading .800 winning percentage, and league-leading 2.42 earned-run average.

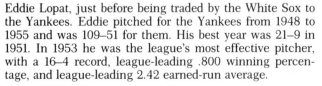

As Arndt Jorgens was to Bill Dickey in the 1930s, so Charlie Silvera was to Yogi Berra in the 1950s. Charlie joined the club in 1948 and stayed until 1956, seldom getting a chance to play. When he did break into the lineup, however, he never embarrassed himself. His busiest year was 1949, when he got into 58 games and batted .315. ➡️

Casey Stengel, in person.

Left to right: Tommy Henrich, Johnny Lindell, and Joe DiMaggio, in 1949.

Frank Hiller, a right-handed pitcher who was with the Yankees from 1946 to 1949. The only time Frank saw any extended action was in 1948, when he was 5–2.

Ralph Houk was on the roster from 1947 to 1954, spending most of his time in the bullpen. Ralph's service was highly infrequent during his playing career—158 at bats in eight years. The Yankees, however, liked his baseball sense and held onto him.

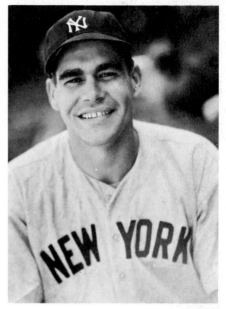

Charlie Keller.

Clubhouse neighbors Joe Page (left) and Joe DiMaggio in a pregame chat at Yankee Stadium in September 1949.

A play at the plate in the fourth game of the 1949 World Series between the Yankees and the Dodgers. Yankees pitcher Ed Lopat is making the dirt fly in Ebbets Field, but Brooklyn's Roy Campanella has the plate expertly blocked as he applies the tag for the putout.

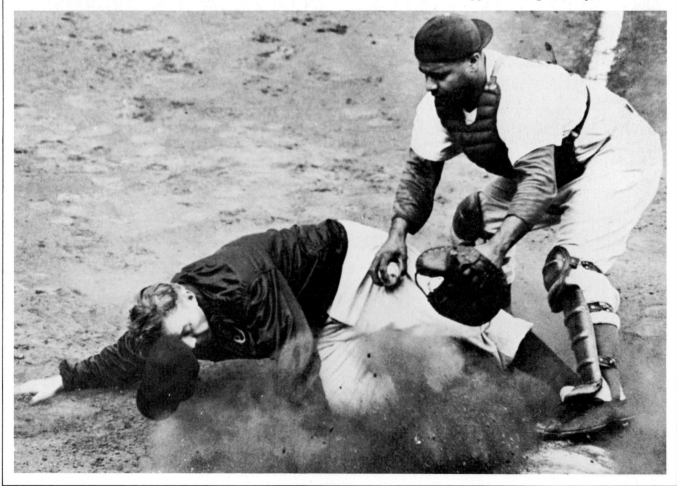

Vic Raschi, considered by many as the Yankees' "money" pitcher in the early 1950s. He was big on the mound, intense, and he threw hard. With the Yankees from 1946 until he was traded to the Cardinals in the spring of 1954, Raschi never had anything resembling a losing season. From 1948 through 1951 his won-lost records were 19–8, 21–10, 21–8, and 21–10. In 1954 he led the league in strikeouts.

Tommy Henrich in 1949.

Five Yankees facing the camera in 1953. Left to right: Berra, Mantle, Collins, Bauer, Woodling.

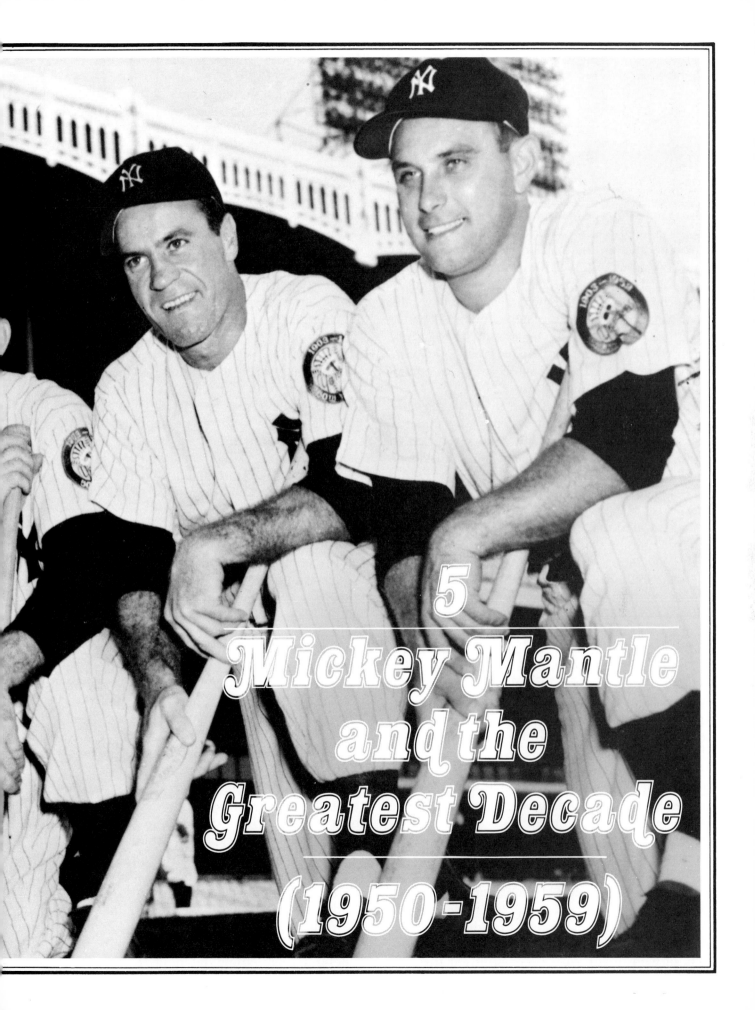

5
Mickey Mantle
and the
Greatest Decade
(1950-1959)

Stengel, who became the third of the great Yankee managers (following Huggins and McCarthy), was a most unlikely candidate for stardom. For one thing, he had behind him an unbroken record of failure as a big-league manager. In previous managerial stints, running the Brooklyn Dodgers from 1934 to 1936 and the Boston Braves from 1938 to 1943, he had finished in the second division nine times out of nine. For another thing, he was considered a clown, hardly the type of man to determine the on-the-field fortunes of the lordly New York Yankees. Well, he was something of a clown, but his was a calculated sort of clowning. It was for the amusement of the fans and the benefit of the writers. Speaking a garbled, sometimes hardly intelligible English when he chose, he could be extremely shrewd and witty. The press loved him. He became the Yankees' most valuable public-relations asset since Babe Ruth.

There were numerous skeptics in the baseball world who were genuinely appalled by the Yankees' choice of a new manager. But Stengel had failed only because his teams had been inept. In life he was a howling success, having invested early and wisely in oil wells and other sterling commercial enterprises. He was also a distinguished banker in Glendale, California.

By the time he was fifty-nine years old and hired by the Yankees, Stengel did not need baseball in order to earn a livelihood. He needed it because it was his life, always had been, always would be. Born in Kansas City, Missouri (his nickname was created out of the city's initials), he came to the big leagues as an outfielder with the 1912 Brooklyn Dodgers. He was a journeyman player, putting in time with the Dodgers, Pirates, Phillies, Giants, and Braves. His big years were 1922 and 1923, when as a part-timer in the Giant outfield he batted .368 and .339, playing for the one manager he always idolized above all others, John McGraw.

Clown he was (doffing his cap to the crowd one day and releasing a bird he had caught), and wisecracker, too. But he was from the beginning one of the game's most astute students, watching, asking questions, never forgetting anything. ("You could look it up," he would say when reciting some obscure episode of a half-century before.) And baseball people—those who did the hiring—knew this. From the time he retired as an active player in 1925 he was seldom without a job as a coach or manager, either in the big leagues or the high minors.

Those who might have been surprised that the dour, humorless Weiss had chosen Stengel as his manager perhaps did not know that the two men went far back together. In 1925 they had been club owners in the Eastern League and had been drawn to one another by their mutual knowledge of the game. Weiss had always respected Stengel's clear, concise analyses; Stengel could speak with crystal clarity when he chose. Weiss knew, too, that despite Casey's apparently nonchalant attitude toward life, the man could be firm and even severe when it came to the demanding business of handling men and winning ball games. Like McGraw, McCarthy, Durocher, and all successful managers, he was indifferent to personal popularity among his players. While some resented his platooning and some resented his antics, few denied his managerial skills.

It was not a particularly great Yankee team with which Stengel began his career in pinstripes. For one thing, the club used seven different first basemen during the 1949 season, with the veteran Henrich playing the bag in 52 games. It was a transitional year, with newcomer Jerry Coleman at second base, and three new faces in the outfield: Gene Woodling, Cliff Mapes, and a tough-looking ex-marine named Hank Bauer. Rizzuto was the only man that year to play in more than 128 games as Stengel shuffled and platooned an injury-ridden club.

Stengel's strength lay on the mound. Along with his three superb front men, Raschi, Reynolds, and Lopat (who averaged 18 wins apiece, Raschi tops with 21), was the flowering of a wild but fast left-hander, Tommy Byrne, who was 15–7 that year. And Joe Page had regained his form, appearing in 60 games, winning 13 and saving 27.

The 1949 season started ominously for the Yankees: the Big Guy was hurt. An agonizingly painful bone spur in his heel incapacitated DiMaggio for the first two months of the season, a season in which the Yankees battled McCarthy's Red Sox down to the final inning of the final game before the pennant was finally decided.

After missing the first 66 games of the season, Joe reported to the team on June 28 in Boston, where the Yankees were starting a three-game series with the Red Sox. What he did in that series ranks second in DiMaggio lore only to his hitting streak. In the first game he singled and homered, the second game he hit two home runs, and the third game he hit another home run. Over the three-game set, which the Yankees swept from the Sox, DiMaggio hit four homers and drove in nine runs.

Behind their strong pitching, DiMaggio's lusty

hitting (Joe ended with a .346 average and 67 RBIs in 76 games), and Stengel's shrewd manipulating of his players, the Yankees fought the Red Sox down to the season's final series, a series which seemed to have evolved out of the head of some Hollywood dream merchant.

Holding a one-game lead, the Red Sox came into Yankee Stadium for Saturday and Sunday games on the season's final weekend. The Yankees took the Saturday game 5–4, behind Page's relief pitching and a game-winning home run by Johnny Lindell in the eighth.

The season's finale remains one of the most memorable games in Yankee history. With the two teams in a first-place deadlock, Stengel sent his ace, Vic Raschi, to the mound. McCarthy countered with Ellis Kinder, riding a 23–5 season. Fittingly, it was a tense, closely played game, with the Yankees taking a 1–0 lead into the last half of the eighth. The New Yorkers then broke it open with four runs, three of them scoring on a humpbacked double by Jerry Coleman which the Red Sox right fielder Al Zarilla barely missed catching. The Red Sox touched Raschi for three in the top of the ninth, but it was a classic case of too little too late.

The Brooklyn Dodgers were back on top in the National League, hoping to avenge their defeats of '41 and '47 and win their first world championship. They did neither. It proved a tame series, with none of the bizarre touches usually attendant on a Brooklyn World Series.

The first game was a sizzling pitching duel between two hard-throwing right-handers, Brooklyn's Don Newcombe and New York's Allie Reynolds. Reynolds allowed just two hits, Newcombe five—the fifth being a leadoff home run by Henrich in the bottom of the ninth, giving the Yankees a 1–0 win. Lefty Preacher Roe returned the 1–0 shutout for Brooklyn in the second game. But thereafter it was the Yankees, quickly and efficiently, winning in five.

The Yankee hero in game three was a familiar National League face transplanted in the American League. Late in the season, the New Yorkers had acquired slugging first baseman Johnny Mize from the Giants in a waiver deal. The thirty-six-year-old Mize remained five years as a part-time first baseman and murderous pinch hitter. In that third game his ninth-inning pinch hit broke up a 1–1 tie and gave the Yankees the game.

It is doubtful if any of his many later championships were as sweet to Stengel as this first one. The "Clown" (he was soon dubbed the "Old Professor" for the zany erudition he brought to his game) had

not only won a close pennant race by beating a Red Sox team with a starting lineup superior to his own, but had then gone on to take the World Series from a Brooklyn team that was also, on paper, superior to his own.

It was easier in 1950, as Stengel led his team to their second straight pennant by three games over Detroit. Rizzuto had his greatest year as a Yankee, batting .324 and being chosen the league's Most Valuable Player. Bauer batted .320, Berra .322 while catching 148 games. DiMaggio, thirty-five years old now, dropped to .301 but still had enough rip left to hit 32 home runs and drive in 122 runs. Mize supplied the team with some exceptionally heavy punch. Playing about half the time at first base, he hit 25 home runs and drove in 72 runs.

The already strong pitching, with Raschi again winning 21, Lopat 18, Reynolds 16, and Byrne 15, was augmented in midseason by a compact, tow-headed, curve-balling twenty-one-year-old left-hander named Edward Charles ("Whitey") Ford. This cocky, supremely confident product of the sidewalks of New York was to become the most outstanding of all Yankee pitchers.

Signed for a bargain-basement $7,000 bonus by the Yankees in 1946 (the Dodgers and Red Sox were interested but decided Whitey was not worth more), Ford had minor-league records of 13–4, 16–8, and 16–5, and was 9–3 at Kansas City when the big team called him up. Coming to the top, with a superb infield behind him to pick up the endless ground balls he threw, Ford was even better. He was 9–1 for his first half-year's work in the big leagues. Also on the club that season was twenty-two-year-old second baseman Billy Martin, whose aggressiveness on the field and brash, unawed personality quickly won him Stengel's affection.

The Philadelphia Phillies had won their first pennant since 1915, but that was the last thing they won in 1950. One could hardly fault the Phillies for going down four straight in the World Series; after all, the four starting pitchers against them were Raschi, Reynolds, Lopat, Ford. In the four games the Phillies got 5 runs and 26 hits. Their own pitching was almost as strong, as the scores 1–0, 2–1, 3–2, and 5–2 attest. The Yankees had just a bit more noise in their bats. DiMaggio broke up the second game with a tenth-inning home run off of the Phillies' great right-hander Robin Roberts.

The Yankees rolled to their third consecutive pennant in 1951 but hardly anyone was paying attention. Baseball interest was riveted upon the National League, as the Dodgers and Giants fought grimly through the waning days of September for the pennant. The scorching race ended in a dead-lock, forcing a three-game play-off which culminated in Bobby Thomson's stunning home run, the single most famous swing of a bat in baseball history.

A game but emotionally drained Giant team fought the Yankees for six games before succumbing. Stengel's men won their third consecutive world championship, but 1951 would always belong to the Giants.

Raschi won 21 for the third straight time, joined by Lopat, who won the same amount, and Reynolds, who won 17. After his brilliant debut, Ford entered the army and was lost to the club for the 1951 and 1952 seasons. Rookie righty Tom Morgan was 9–3. The Yankees made a good midseason pickup in a trade with Washington, a left-handed relief pitcher named Bob Kuzava; and in late August they obtained from the Boston Braves the veteran right-handed curve baller Johnny Sain, who was a fine asset in the Yankee bullpen over the next few years. To get him, however, they paid a higher price than they perhaps realized—$50,000 and a young right-hander from their farm system who would have a fine career in the National League and come back to haunt them later. His name was Lew Burdette.

On July 12, 1951, Reynolds pitched a no-hitter against the Indians, the first such effort by a Yankee pitcher since Monte Pearson no-hit the Indians in 1938. It was the fifth no-hitter in Yankee history, the previous ones being hurled by Tom Hughes in 1910, George Mogridge in 1917, and Sam Jones in 1923. Reynolds came back on September 28 and fired another hitless game against a hard-hitting Red Sox team at the Stadium. This game had perhaps the most dramatic ending of any no-hitter ever pitched. With two out in the ninth, Reynolds found himself confronted by the game's greatest hitter, Ted Williams. Reynolds got Ted to lift a foul behind the plate. Berra, normally so sure-handed, had some trouble with the ball and dropped it. Reynolds went back to the mound with the thankless task of trying to retire Williams twice in the same at bat. Allie fired another blazer and again Williams popped it up behind the plate. This time Berra caught it.

That 1951 season was in many ways a significant and symbolic one for the Yankees. In December, a baseball-weary, thirty-seven-year-old DiMaggio announced his retirement. The aches and pains were coming more frequently and leaving more slowly. There had been a marked erosion of his once peerless skills. Playing in 116 games, he had seen his average drop to .263, his home runs to 12. They were throwing the fast ball past him now. He could have stayed on for another year and collected his $100,000 salary; in fact, Topping and Webb wanted him to. But that same burning pride that had helped make him the greatest player of his era would not allow him to stay on when he could no longer perform up to his own exacting standards.

But even as they were losing their long-time star and drawing card, the Yankees were about to give the rest of baseball an object lesson in how to perpetuate a dynasty. The farm system was turning out more players than the top team could absorb. Among them were the versatile Gil McDougald, who played all around the infield for ten years; outfielder Jackie Jensen, whom they would trade and who would become one of the league's premier sluggers; power-hitting outfielder Bob Cerv, who could not break into the lineup; and the jewel of the organization, the nineteen-year-old switch-hitting Mickey Mantle.

Mantle was born to be a ballplayer; he was trained to be one by his father, and he was even named for one—his father's favorite, Mickey Cochrane. No player ever possessed as much raw, natural talent as did this muscular, Oklahoma-born youngster. He had awesome power from either side of the plate, stunning speed afoot, and a strong throwing arm. Only a career-long series of injuries—knee injuries, shoulder problems, broken bones, pulled muscles—kept him from rewriting the record book and posting an even more impressive career history than he did.

He was signed in June 1949 by one of those relentless Yankee scouts, Tom Greenwade, for a bonus of around $1,100 and a $400 contract to play out the season with the Yankees' Independence, Missouri, farm club in the Class-D Kansas-Oklahoma-Missouri (K-O-M) League. Mickey batted .313 and hit seven home runs in 89 games. He was a shortstop then and apparently his vast skills did not extend to picking up ground balls or throwing them accurately, for he made 47 errors in his 89 games.

The following year he was promoted to Class-C ball, playing with the Joplin, Missouri, team. He batted a league-leading .383 that year, hitting 26 home runs and driving in 136 runs in 137 games. Still a shortstop, he made 55 errors.

Such was the beginning of a career that ended in the Hall of Fame. Along the way there were those titanic home runs called "tape measures," a Triple Crown, three Most Valuable Player Awards, and a career total of 536 home runs. As DiMaggio had replaced Ruth in the Yankee pantheon, so Mantle replaced DiMaggio, becoming one of the game's premier gate attractions. But in the spring of 1951 he was still just a hard-swinging, error-prone short-stop who had so far played no higher than C ball.

It is doubtful if Mickey ever received even a moment's consideration from the Yankees as a shortstop. It wasn't just all those errors; there was also a gentleman named Rizzuto, fresh from having been named the league's Most Valuable Player.

Once Stengel got an eyeful of the shy, retiring youngster's power from either side of the plate, he was determined to keep Mantle with the Yankees, even though the leap from Class-C to the big leagues was in virtual defiance of baseball's gravitational laws. In addition, the New York writers were filing such laudatory, adjective-strewn stories about him all spring that Mantle was something of a celebrity even before the team reached New York.

Mickey was in the Yankees' opening-day lineup in 1951, playing right field. His initial progress was slow and uncertain and by midseason he had been demoted to the Yankees' Kansas City farm club. There, in forty games, he hit .361 with 11 home runs and 50 runs batted in. He was soon back in New York; not even the Yankees were so lavishly stocked with talent that they could allow a Mantle to remain down on the farm very long. Mickey returned and finished the season with a .267 average, playing right field alongside DiMaggio in center.

In the 1951 World Series against the Giants, Mantle suffered the first of the many injuries that haunted his career. In the fifth inning of the second game, he and DiMaggio converged on a fly ball to right center. Running at top speed, Mickey stepped on a drain cover and went sprawling across the Yankee Stadium grass. He was finished for the series, his right knee badly sprained.

Historians later noted that the fly ball had been hit by the Giants' own spectacular rookie, center fielder Willie Mays, against whom Mantle was weighed and measured on many a New York City street corner and saloon for years to come.

Of the 1952 season, Eddie Lopat remembered, "We soon learned we had better not make any plans for October." Not that the fourth straight pennant was any picnic; DiMaggio was gone, and into the service went infielders Bobby Brown and Jerry Coleman and pitcher Tom Morgan. In addition, Lopat was hampered by a bad arm and missed almost half his starts.

But there was still talent on the roster and Stengel manipulated it beautifully all year. Billy Martin took over at second and Gil McDougald, whose versatility

was priceless, gave the New Yorkers a steady game at third. The outfield was solid, with Mantle batting .311 in his first full season, Woodling .309, and Bauer .293. Berra, catching 140 games, led the club with 30 home runs and 98 runs batted in.

Reynolds was 1952's big winner with a 20–8 record; Raschi was 16–6, Sain 11–6, and Lopat 10–5. It was a good staff, though it could not compare with Cleveland's three 20-game winners, Bob Lemon, Early Wynn, and Mike Garcia. Nevertheless, the Yankees edged the Indians by two games in a hard-fought race.

That October, the Yankees won an unprecedented fourth straight world championship, defeating a powerful Brooklyn team in seven games. The pay-off game was saved in the seventh inning when Billy Martin made a spectacular grab of a pop fly. It should have been a routine out; the bases were loaded and there were two out when Jackie Robinson lifted a pop-up not far behind the mound. There was indecision in the Yankee infield. Martin, always alert on a ball field, saw that no one was moving for the ball and came dashing in to take it just before it hit the grass, with Dodgers wheeling around the bases the whole time. The Yankees, leading 4–2 at the time, took the game and the series.

The '53 Yankees salted their record-breaking fifth straight pennant with an 18-game winning streak early in the season (one short of the league record held by the 1906 White Sox and '47 Yankees). Fifteen of those wins were achieved on the road; it was the Yankees' way of traveling around the league and telling each club to forget it.

Stengel made the record books that year and he did it without a 20-game winner. His ace that year, and for many more to come, was Whitey Ford, just back from the service, who put together an 18–6 record. Whitey was soon to join Mantle and Martin to form the game's most famous and carefree off-the-field triumvirate. Martin, who was Stengel's favorite, was looked upon less favorably by Weiss, who felt Billy to be a dubious influence on the other two. On Mantle perhaps, but it is doubtful that Martin or anyone else could have misled Ford, a sharp city slicker (indeed, Mantle's nickname for his buddy was "Slick"). Behind Ford were the veteran left-hander Lopat, back from his miseries with a 16–4 record; Sain, 14–7; Raschi, 13–6; and Reynolds, 13–7. It was one of the finest Yankee staffs ever.

The club's .273 average was good enough to lead the league, but there were no big bangers that year. Woodling's .306 led the team. Mantle batted .295

with 21 home runs. One of those clouts made history. It came off left-hander Chuck Stobbs in old Griffith Stadium in Washington and was estimated to have traveled some 565 feet. The writers called it "Ruthian"—the Babe was still the yardstick for such things.

For the fourth time in seven years it was a Yankee-Dodger World Series. This time it went six games and the Yankees won their fifth consecutive world championship, one of the most stunning achievements by any team in any sport.

New York's heroics came from an unlikely source, as is apt to be the case in a World Series. Billy Martin, a .257 hitter during the season, went on a tear during those early October days, getting 12 hits in 24 at bats for a .500 average. Included in Billy's mayhem against Dodger pitching were two home runs, two triples, a double, and eight runs batted in. His last RBI came on a ground-ball single in the bottom of the ninth of the sixth game, breaking a tie that had come in the top of the inning on a dramatic two-run homer by Carl Furillo.

The Yankees were on top of the world like no team in baseball had ever been. Even more than the 1926–1928 or 1936–1939 Yankee teams, they dominated the game. And when defeat finally came, as it did in 1954, it came in a season when they won 103 games.

The year Stengel did not win the pennant was in many ways his finest performance. There was a lot of age on his pitching staff: Lopat was thirty-six, Reynolds thirty-nine, Sain thirty-six. And that spring Stengel's clutch pitcher, Raschi, was sold to the Cardinals after a bitter salary dispute with Weiss. (Stengel had no voice in the deal and was chagrined when he heard of it.)

Ford was 16–8 that year, Reynolds 13–4 (it was his last time around, as a back injury forced his retirement), Lopat 12–4 (Steady Eddie, too, was gone by midseason the next year). Picking up the staff was another farm product, right-hander Bob Grim, who posted a 20–6 record starting and relieving.

The Yankees had four .300 hitters in the lineup: Mantle, .300; Berra, .307; Irv Noren, .319; and rookie third baseman Andy Carey, .302. Except for the thirty-six-year-old Rizzuto, who slumped to .195, it was a strong lineup, good enough to lead the league again in batting.

Despite registering his highest win total ever as a Yankee manager, Stengel saw his club's reign put to an end by Al Lopez's Cleveland Indians, whose torrid club won 111 games, one more than the league record set by the '27 Yankees. A solid if unspectacular club in the field, Cleveland did it with one of the great pitching staffs of all time. Bob Lemon and Early Wynn won 23 apiece, Mike Garcia 19, Art Houtteman 15, an aging but still effective Bob Feller 13. And in the bullpen, Lopez had a pair of stoppers in righty Ray Narleski and lefty Don Mossi.

Concerned with the age on their pitching staff, the Yankees swung a man-sized deal with the Baltimore Orioles that November that brought them two strong young right arms. The Orioles, in their second year in the league, were in need of ball-players. (The Orioles had been formerly the St. Louis Browns, the franchise shift being the league's first since 1903, when Baltimore dropped out to be replaced by New York.) The Yankees sent Baltimore, among others, outfielder Gene Woodling, pitchers Jim McDonald and Harry Byrd, and catchers Hal Smith and Gus Triandos. In return they received shortstop Billy Hunter and pitchers Bob Turley and Don Larsen.

Larsen went on to make baseball history, but Turley was the key man for the Yankees. The burly righty could fire as hard as anyone. He had won 14 for a seventh-place team and led the league in strikeouts. Larsen had been saddled with an ignominious 3–21 record, but Stengel liked what he had seen of the big guy.

In addition to the new pitchers, the Yankees felt they had at last found their regular first baseman. Incredibly, they had been without a solidly established first baseman since Gehrig's retirement fifteen years before. It was not for lack of trying. During those years the following men had appeared, for better or worse, at first base: Babe Dahlgren, Johnny Sturm, Jerry Priddy, Buddy Hassett, Ed Levy, Nick Etten, Johnny Lindell, Steve Souchok, George McQuinn, Jack Phillips, Tommy Henrich, Billy Johnson, Dick Kryhoski, Fenton Mole, Johnny Mize, Johnny Hopp, Hank Workman, Joe DiMaggio (one game), Irv Noren, Don Bollweg, Gus Triandos, Eddie Robinson, Frank Leja, and Joe Collins. Collins, an able performer, had been more or less the regular the past few years, but Joe was a lifetime .256 hitter. The new man was Bill ("Moose") Skowron. He had hit .340 as a part-timer in 1954, and in 1955, still platooning with Collins, he batted .319. A right-handed hitter, Skowron had good power to right and right-center, where he was to plant many of his home runs.

The Yankees rose to the top again in 1955, beating out Cleveland by three games. Mantle batted .306

and led the league with 37 home runs. Berra won the MVP Award for the third time, catching 145 games and driving in 108 runs. Ford topped the staff with an 18–7 record, while Turley in his first year in pinstripes was 17–13. Tommy Byrne, back after having been exiled for several years, was 16–5. Larsen, who almost didn't win the year before, almost didn't lose this time, with a 9–2 record. Grim, a 20-game winner the year before, saw arm trouble reduce his record to 7–5.

There was another addition to the Yankee team in 1955, a notable one in more ways than one. It had been eight years since Jackie Robinson had broken the color line with the Dodgers, and eight years since Larry Doby had joined Cleveland to become the American League's first black player. Meanwhile the Yankees, deaf to growing criticism, had remained lily white. With more and more blacks coming to the big leagues every year, the Yankees' phalanx of twenty-five white faces was becoming more conspicuous. The club's official line was that they were "waiting for the right man." What precisely were the qualities required of this impeccable man were left undefined. (The Yankees were not the worst offenders, though; Tom Yawkey's Red Sox were not integrated until 1959.)

When the Yankees finally did place a black on their roster he possessed in abundance those qualities the team seemed to have been hoping for. He was soft-spoken, reserved, a man of dignity. More important, he was a man of formidable talent, one who could catch and play the outfield, one who could hit and hit with power. His name was Elston Howard. Primarily an outfielder in 1955, the new man brought integration to the Yankees along with a .290 batting average.

Optimistic as ever, the Brooklyn Dodgers showed up once more that October, hoping that this, their eighth World Series, would finally give them their long-sought championship. When the Yankees took the first two games in the Stadium it seemed like old times. But then the Dodgers surged back and took three in a row at Ebbets Field. Ford four-hit the Brooks back at the Stadium, setting the table for a seventh game.

Byrne hooked up with a young left-handed fast baller, Johnny Podres, who had beaten Turley in game three. It was Johnny's day, and it was Brooklyn's year. Podres shut out the Yankees 2–0, with the help of a breathtaking catch by left fielder Sandy Amoros. Amoros's catch—it remains a phrase by itself in baseball history—broke the back of a Yankee rally in the sixth inning, turning what

looked like a game-tying extra base hit by Berra into a double play. It was the Yankees' first series loss after seven straight wins, dating back to 1942.

Led by Mantle, who had his greatest season in 1956, the Yanks easily outdistanced the Indians, despite the presence of three 20-gamers on Lopez's staff (Wynn, Lemon, and sophomore sensation Herb Score). It was Mickey's Triple Crown season, and only the sixth time in American League history that a player had achieved the distinction of leading the league in home runs, runs batted in, and batting average. (The previous winners were Ty Cobb in 1909, Jimmy Foxx in 1933, Lou Gehrig in 1934, and Ted Williams in 1942 and 1947.) In winning his Triple Crown, Mantle batted .353, hit 52 home runs, and drove in 130 runs. His 52 home runs put him in very elite company indeed; only three other American Leaguers, Ruth (four times), Foxx (twice), and Greenberg, had attained the 50 mark in home runs.

Nineteen fifty-six was an old-fashioned power year for the New Yorkers. Along with Mickey's 52 long ones, Berra hit 30, Bauer 26, and Skowron 23. Overall the team hit 190 home runs. Skowron batted .308; McDougald, the shortstop after the midyear release of the veteran Rizzuto, hit .311.

Ford, again almost unbeatable, was 19–6. He was backed up by sophomore right-hander Johnny Kucks, who was 18–9 (it was a magic Johnny proved unable to repeat), and newcomer Tom Sturdivant, who was 16–8. Larsen was 11–5 while Turley slumped off to 8–4.

Once more the Brooklyn Dodgers showed up in October. If the rest of the world was beginning to think the World Series was an exclusively New York show, one could hardly wonder; of a total of 16 pennants won since 1951, 14 had gone to New York teams. The series again went seven games, but this time the Yankees emerged on top, reclaiming the championship they had loaned to Brooklyn the year before.

In game two Stengel sent Larsen to the mound, but not for long; the big guy was out by the second inning. But in game five he was perfect—literally. Facing baseball's most awesome lineup, he retired twenty-seven Dodgers in a row, pitching the only perfect game in series history. Working out of a no-windup delivery, Larsen worked with remorseless efficiency, reducing the Dodgers to utter helplessness with only ninety-seven pitches. In the second inning Jackie Robinson hit a line drive off of Carey's glove at third, but McDougald picked up the ball and threw Jackie out. In the fifth Gil Hodges hit a long drive to deep left-center, which Mantle backhanded.

That was as close as the Dodgers came to spoiling Larsen's day. The final batter was pinch hitter Dale Mitchell, a former .300 batter with Cleveland, who was called out on strikes. "It was a foot outside," Mitchell groused later.

In the 1927 World Series against Pittsburgh, Herb Pennock had retired the first twenty-two men he faced, losing both no-hitter and perfect game with one out in the eighth. In 1939 Monte Pearson also had a no-hitter until one out in the eighth, against Cincinnati. In 1947 Bill Bevens went until two out in the ninth before giving up his famous hit to Lavagetto. In 1956 Don Larsen went all the way and then some.

The following day, Brooklyn's Clem Labine shut out Turley and the Yankees 1–0 in an 11-inning beauty. But the day after that Kucks put the icing on a fine season for himself and his mates with a 9–0 whitewashing for another Yankee championship.

By 1957 there had been another franchise shift: the Philadelphia Athletics were in Kansas City, the Yankees relinquishing their territorial rights in order to allow the move. But Kansas City, it soon became evident, did not cease being a Yankee farm team. Arnold Johnson, the wealthy Chicago businessman who owned the Kansas City Athletics, was a baseball innocent. Johnson soon came under the influence of the Yankees, who began a series of trades with the A's that was reminiscent of the infamous rape of the Red Sox years before. There were stories that Johnson and Del Webb had business interests outside of baseball that made Johnson beholden. There were stories that Weiss had some of Johnson's front-office people in his pocket. Or maybe it was simply that the Kansas City people were gullible. Whatever the reason, the traffic between New York and Kansas City was steady and scandalous. Such was the power that Del Webb quietly wielded behind the scenes in those years that Commissioner Ford Frick, a compliant sort anyway, averted his glance and allowed the deals to go on.

In February 1957 the Yankees sent six players to K.C., the most notable being pitcher Tom Morgan, shortstop Billy Hunter, and outfielder Irv Noren. In return they received right-handed pitcher Art Ditmar, left-hander Bobby Shantz, and a twenty-year-old third baseman named Clete Boyer, whom the A's had given a large bonus to sign. In June the Yankees acquired from Kansas City a nearsighted right-hander with an overpowering fast ball, Ryne Duren, who became a sensational relief pitcher for several years, and outfielder Harry ("Suitcase") Simpson. In exchange they sent promising young right-hander Ralph Terry, Billy Martin, and two other players. The lovely part of this deal is that two years later, when Terry began to mature as a pitcher, the Athletics promptly dealt him back.

Getting rid of Martin had not been Stengel's idea. Weiss, who had never liked Billy very much, finally saw his chance to rid the club of what he believed was a detrimental influence. Martin and some of his teammates had been out on the town to celebrate his and Berra's birthdays, which came a few days apart in mid-May. The group, which included Mantle, Ford, Bauer, McDougald, and Kucks, went to the Copacabana nightclub. When the smoke cleared there were assault charges, headlines, police, and a ticket to K.C. for Billy, even though Bauer was the man accused of having bashed a delicatessen owner from the Bronx. The case was eventually thrown out of court.

What really happened that memorable night at the Copa has been lost to the imprecise recollections of history, but in all probability Bauer and his mates were innocent of having committed any mayhem. Berra, an honest man and unimpeachable witness, said, "Nobody did nothin' to nobody." Nevertheless, Weiss moved against Martin and Billy began his journey along a long road that eventually led back to Yankee Stadium and a different glory. Lest one think Weiss would trade his regular second baseman out of sheer spite, bear in mind that the Yankee farm system had just coughed up a second sacker named Bobby Richardson, eight years younger than Billy, a better ballplayer, and a proper churchgoing gentleman.

Otherwise 1957 was standard fare in Yankee history. Mantle reached his batting peak with a .365 average, but failed to win the batting crown because the thirty-eight-year-old Ted Williams batted .388. Skowron, Richardson, McDougald, and Carey gave the New Yorkers a young, solid infield. Another new face belonged to a twenty-year-old rookie named Tony Kubek, whose ability to play the infield and outfield with equal adeptness and poke the ball in the clutch delighted Stengel. The Yankee roster was becoming so crowded with talent that Kubek, Howard, Coleman, and another fine rookie, Jerry Lumpe, had to sit on the bench much of the time.

Ford, bothered with arm trouble, dropped to 11–5 but Turley, Sturdivant, Grim, Shantz, Larsen, and Ditmar all pitched winning ball and the Yankees came in eight games ahead of the White Sox. Al Lopez had switched from Cleveland to Chicago, but second place was still his lot. Al was destined to finish second 10 times during his managerial career, nine of those times behind the Yankees.

In the 1957 series an old face came back to haunt the Yankees. Lew Burdette, whom the Yanks had dispatched in 1951 to the Braves for Johnny Sain, was a Milwaukee ace and proved it by hurling three complete-game victories against his former employers, two of them shutouts. Lew and the Braves won it in seven.

By 1958 the Yankees had New York all to themselves, the Dodgers and Giants having taken wagons west to dig for California gold. They also had the American League all to themselves as they took a fourth straight pennant, finishing 10 games ahead of Lopez's White Sox.

Turley blazed to a 21–7 Cy Young Award year. It was Bullet Bob's greatest season. Ford continued to double his losses with wins, going 14–7. They were the only double-digit winners as Casey's boys won only 92 games, Stengel's lowest win total but more than enough that year.

Kubek was the regular shortstop, the versatile McDougald was at second, and Skowron and Carey anchored the corners, with Howard, Lumpe, and Richardson getting a game when they could. Mantle and his 42 home runs shared the outfield with Bauer and young Norm Siebern, who batted .300 in his first full season. The farm system was still sending players, as was Kansas City. A midseason deal brought New York right-hander Duke Maas in exchange for Grim and Simpson. Suitcase hadn't cut it with the Yankees in his brief time and there were no second chances in those years.

The 1958 World Series was an exciting one. Milwaukee was back, but this time Lew Burdette's magic was wanting. It was a close one, however. Down three games to one, the New Yorkers came storming back to take three straight, thanks to some muscular pitching by Turley. Bauer tied a series record, stunning the Braves with four home runs. The key blow, however, was a three-run clout by Skowron in the eighth inning of game seven, which iced a 6–2 win and another world-championship flag for the Yankee Stadium winds to caress.

Stengel began the 1959 season in full expectation of tying his own record with another clutch of five straight pennants. The Old Man had taken nine out of ten and become, next to Emmett Kelly, America's most respected clown. But this was the year that his most tenacious pursuer, Al Lopez, once again proved that if you knock on a door long enough someone will finally open it. If not for the pushy Lopez, the Yankees would have captured sixteen straight pennants between 1949 and 1964, a record that might have embarrassed even the New Yorkers.

Not only did the Yankees not win in '59, they dropped to third place, their first time since 1948 in a slot that some teams don't reach for decades. They were 15 games out, trailing the winning White Sox and Indians.

The club hit well, but not as well as the year before. Mantle dropped to .285; Bauer, near the end now, saw his average shrink to .238. Siebern fell to .271. Skowron, Richardson, Kubek, and that Gibraltar behind the plate, Berra, had respectable seasons.

In need of pitching, the club again looked west. Deciding that Ralph Terry had sufficiently matured on the mound, they reacquired him from Kansas City for a sore-armed Sturdivant, a fading Kucks, and the solid Jerry Lumpe, for whom there was no room on the club. Along with Terry came Hector Lopez, a good-hit, no-field infielder-outfielder.

On December 17 the Yankees again raided the K.C. roster, and this time they hit the jackpot. In return for Bauer, Siebern, the no-longer effective Larsen, and first baseman Marv Thorneberry (who found fame elsewhere in New York a few years later), they obtained the man who was shortly to break Babe Ruth's single-season home-run record.

Phil Rizzuto, the American League's Most Valuable Player in 1950.

Cliff Mapes, who was in the outfield for the Yankees from 1948 to 1951. Mapes was a big man, with power and a strong throwing arm, but he never quite made it with the Yankees; his highest average was .247.

Second baseman Jerry Coleman, a dazzling glove man and a steady hitter. Coleman was with the Yankees from 1949 to 1957, with some time out when he was recalled to active service during the Korean War. His best years were his first two, when he batted .275 and .287. When it came to making the double play it was said that Coleman had no peer.

The 1950 outfield. Left to right: Joe DiMaggio, Hank Bauer, Gene Woodling.

An airborne Coleman has just fired on to first base to complete a double play. The base runner is Jerry Scala of the White Sox. The action occurred at Chicago's Comiskey Park on June 14, 1950.

A happy group of Yankees riding the rails in 1950.

Hank Bauer, a big favorite at Yankee Stadium from 1948 to 1959. He was a good outfielder, a nonstop hustler, a strong hitter, and was as tough as he looks. Hank's best year was 1950, when he batted .320. In '53 he batted .304 and on three other occasions went over the .290 mark. He hit four home runs in the 1958 World Series, tying a then-existing record.

Gene Woodling, who swung out of this modified Stan Musial–type stance, joined the Yankees in 1949 and remained with them until 1954, one of their most dependable players. In 1952 and 1953 he put together his two best years as a Yankee, with batting averages of .309 and .306. In five World Series, Gene batted .318.

Tommy Byrne, a left-hander with a lot of whimsy and a lot of smoke on his fast ball. Byrne, sometimes quite wild but most of the time quite effective, joined the Yankees in 1943, returned in 1946, was traded in 1951 and returned again in 1954, remaining until the end of his career in 1957. In 1949 and 1950 he was 15–7 and 15–9, and in 1955 he had the league's top winning percentage of .762 on a 16–5 record.

Outfielder Jackie Jensen was with the Yankees from 1950 to 1952, when he was traded to Washington. He was subsequently traded to the Red Sox, where he became one of the league's top sluggers. He batted .298 for the Yankees in 1951.

Tom Ferrick, a journeyman relief pitcher who gave the Yankees one excellent year in 1950, winning 8 and losing 4, after being acquired from the Browns. He was dealt to Washington early the next season in a trade for pitcher Bob Kuzava.

Lew Burdette, a Yankee in the spring of 1950. He was traded to the Braves in a deal for Johnny Sain. Sain helped the Yankees to a few pennants; Burdette went on to win over 200 games in a long career. He beat the Yankees three times in the 1957 World Series.

Joseph Edward Kollonige, better known to Yankee fans as Joe Collins. Joe played first base and some outfield for the team from 1948 to 1957. He was pretty much the regular first baseman in the early 1950s. Joe's best year was 1951, when he batted .286. His home-run high was 18 the following year.

Johnny Mize, the long-time National League slugger whom the Yankees obtained on waivers from the Giants in August 1949. Mize was with the Yankees from 1949 to 1953, helping them to their five consecutive pennants and world championships. He was a part-time first baseman and devastating pinch hitter.

Edward Charles ("Whitey") Ford, greatest pitcher in Yankee history. He led the league three times in wins, three times in winning percentage, twice in earned-run average, and twice in shutouts. His lifetime record is 236–106; his lifetime winning percentage of .690 is the highest of any pitcher with 200 or more wins.

Four members of the 1950 pennant winners. Left to right: Phil Rizzuto, Joe Di-Maggio, Yogi Berra, Jerry Coleman.

These are not twins; it is nineteen-year-old Mickey Charles Mantle, a new man in the Yankees' 1951 spring-training camp, getting ready to become the most powerful switch hitter the game has ever known.

Gil McDougald, another rookie who made the club in 1951. Gil spent his entire big-league career (1951–1960) with the Yankees. His versatility made him invaluable—he was a smooth glove at second, short, or third. He batted .306 in his rookie year and .311 in 1956, his career high.

Tom Morgan also joined the Yankees in 1951, where he pitched from 1951 to 1956. He was 9–3 in '51 and 11–5 in '54, his best year. Stengel used him primarily in relief.

Irv Noren, a left-handed-hitting outfielder the Yankees obtained in 1952 from Washington in a trade involving Jackie Jensen and Spec Shea. Noren played for the Yankees until traded to Kansas City in 1957. His peak year in New York was 1954, when he batted .319.

Eddie Lopat in the early 1950s.

Curve-ball specialist Johnny Sain started and relieved for the Yankees from 1951 to 1955, after having been obtained from the Boston Braves late in the '51 season. Johnny was 11–6 in '52 and 14–7 the next year.

The torch is passed: Joe DiMaggio (left) played his last year in 1951, Mickey Mantle his first. Mickey was nineteen, Joe closing in on thirty-seven.

Casey Stengel (right) and his great trio of starters. Left to right: Allie Reynolds, Vic Raschi, Eddie Lopat.

The Giants, too, had a rookie outfielder that year, and he showed up for the 1951 World Series against the Yankees. Giants manager Leo Durocher (left) and Willie Mays.

During and after. Top: the Giants' Monte Irvin sets sail on a steal of home in the first inning of the first game of the 1951 World Series at Yankee Stadium. Yogi Berra has just received an Allie Reynolds fast ball and batter Bobby Thomson has fallen away to give Irvin room. Bottom: Irvin has slid across—safely, according to umpire Bill Summers. Berra put up a futile argument. Bobby Thomson remains an interested spectator.

Mantle has just collapsed after tripping on a loose drain cover in the Stadium outfield in game two of the 1951 series. Joe DiMaggio, having just caught Willie Mays's fly ball (which both he and Mickey had been pursuing), is coming over to help.

With a badly sprained knee, Mickey was not getting up, as his concerned teammates come running out to assist. No. 29 is Charlie Silvera, No. 32 Ralph Houk, who had been in the bullpen in right field, not far from where Mickey went down. DiMaggio is bending over Mantle.

Game three of the 1951 World Series, at the Polo Grounds. The Giants' Eddie Stanky, who had walked with one out in the bottom of the fifth, attempted a steal of second. He was clearly thrown out, Berra to Rizzuto, but Stanky kicked the ball out of Rizzuto's glove, got up and went on to third. It was a critical play, opening the gates for a five-run Giants rally that gave them the game, 6–2. It was either a dirty play or an aggressive one, depending on your point of view.

Allie Reynolds (left) and Hank Bauer in May 1952. That's a cricket bat Bauer is holding.

Game five of the 1951 World Series, at the Polo Grounds. The score was 1–1 in the third inning, the Yankees had the bases loaded and two out. Giants pitcher Larry Jansen threw it and the Yankees' Gil McDougald hit it—into the left-field stands for a grand-slam home run.

Bob Kuzava, a well-traveled left-hander who made a stop in New York in the middle of his career. Obtained from Washington in 1951, Bob remained with the Yankees until 1954. Used primarily in relief, he gave the club some very efficient work.

Manager Stengel is checking out the style of twenty-year-old rookie third baseman Andy Carey at the spring-training camp in St. Petersburg in March 1952. Signed for a large bonus, Carey was with the Yankees from 1952 to 1960. The youngster became a regular in 1954 and batted .302, his highest mark as a Yankee. Carey was a first-rate defensive player.

Mickey Mantle (left) and Brooklyn's Pee Wee Reese during the 1952 World Series.

Big John Mize whacking one in game five of the 1952 series at Yankee Stadium. With two men on, the Dodgers' Carl Erskine threw John a fat one and the big man drove it into the lower stands in right. The blow capped a five-run Yankee rally in the fifth inning. Erskine stayed in, however, retiring the last 19 men he faced as Brooklyn won it in the eleventh inning, 6–5.

This picture (autographed by Phil Rizzuto) shows Yankee second baseman Billy Martin making his dramatic running grab of Jackie Robinson's infield pop in the seventh inning of the seventh game of the 1952 series. Robinson is running down the line in the foreground; in the background is Phil Rizzuto.

Casey Stengel dispensing some wisdom in game seven of the 1952 series at Ebbets Field.

Four happy Yankees reflect the joy of winning the 1952 World Series. Top: Yogi Berra and Mickey Mantle; bottom: Allie Reynolds and Vic Raschi.

Billy Martin, who has uttered many a mouthful, is here about to consume one. This picture was taken in a New York City restaurant in March 1956.

Casey Stengel and the young infielder who was probably his favorite player, Billy Martin. Martin was with the Yankees from 1950 until he was traded to Kansas City early in the 1957 season. Billy's best years in New York were '52 and '56, when he batted .267 and .264. Never a star ballplayer, Martin was at his best under pressure, as his World Series lifetime batting average of .333 attests. In 28 series games he drove in 19 runs.

Billy Martin firing to first to complete a double play. The base runner is Detroit's Harvey Kuenn, the umpire Ed Hurley. The action occurred on August 6, 1953, at Yankee Stadium.

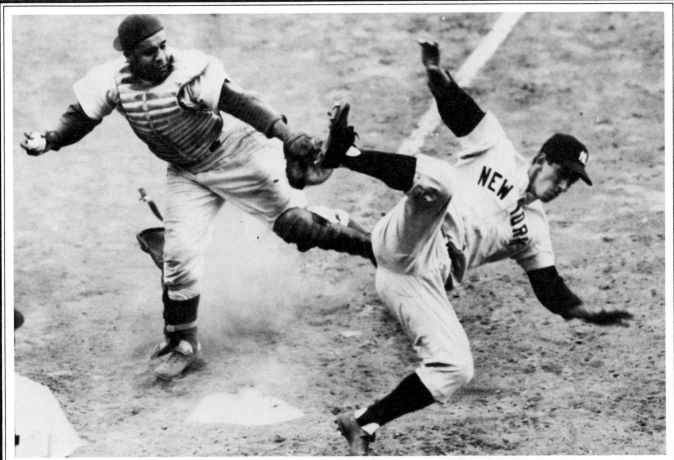

Billy Martin taking a flyer as the last out in game four of the 1953 World Series at Ebbets Field. He was trying to score on Mantle's single, but Brooklyn catcher Roy Campanella tagged him out, and booted him good-by—or so it seems.

Billy Martin in the Yankee clubhouse moments after his base hit in the bottom of the ninth inning of game six gave the Yankees the 1953 championship. It was a fitting ending to a series that saw Martin tie a record by getting 12 hits.

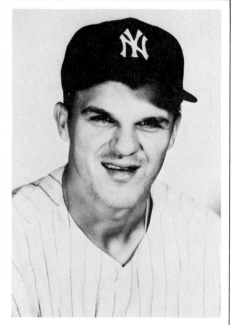

(Top left)
Al Rosen, star Cleveland third base-man of the 1950s who later became president of the Yankees.

(Top center)
Bob Grim, a right-handed pitcher who surprised everyone with a 20–6 record in his rookie year, 1954. He never repeated that suc-cess, his next best year being 1958, when he was 12–8. After his first year, Grim was used primarily as a relief pitcher. He was traded to Kansas City in 1958.

(Top right)
Joining the Yankees in 1954, Bill ("Moose") Skowron became the club's best first baseman since Gehrig. Bill started out for the Yankees with batting averages of .340, .319, 308, and .304. He added another .300 season in 1960 with .309. A man with good power, Bill's home-run high was 28 in 1961. He was traded to the Los Angeles Dodgers after the 1962 season.

After Johnny Mize retired in 1953, the Yankees picked up Eddie Robinson, another veteran long-ball-hitting first baseman, hoping he would fill Mize's shoes. Eddie responded well in 1954, batting .261 and leading the league in pinch hits with 15. He slumped off after that, however, and was traded to Kansas City in 1956.

(Top left)
One of the most physically strong men ever to play big-league baseball, outfielder Bob Cerv came up to the Yankees in 1951 and was with them until 1956, when he was traded to Kansas City. He was back with the team from 1960 to 1962. Never a regular in New York, Cerv performed well when he was able to break into the lineup, batting .341 in 1955 and .304 in 1956.

(Top center)
Herb Score, Cleveland's brilliant young left-hander, was struck in the eye by a line drive off the bat of Gil McDougald in a Yankee-Indian game early in May 1957. Although he recovered, Score was never the same pitcher afterward.

(Top right)
Billy Hunter, Yankees back-up shortstop in 1955 and 1956. He was traded to Kansas City in 1957.

Elston Howard, the Yankees' first black player. Howard played for the Yankees from 1955 to 1967, returning later as a coach. Elston gave the club solid service both in the outfield and behind the plate, becoming the regular catcher in the early 1960s. Howard batted .314 in 1958 and .313 in 1964, but had his biggest year at the plate in 1961, when he batted .348. In 1963, the year he was voted the American League's Most Valuable Player, he hit his career high of 28 home runs.

Mickey Mantle.

Phil Rizzuto in 1956, a few weeks before his unconditional release by the Yankees brought an end to his big-league career.

Don Larsen delivering the ninety-seventh and final pitch of his perfect game against the Dodgers in the 1956 World Series. Billy Martin is in the background.

Don Larsen, the perfect man. He pitched for the Yankees for five years, from 1955 to 1959. In and out because of arm problems during those years, he nevertheless was a consistent, if not big, winner. In his first three years in pinstripes his won-lost records were 9–2, 11–5, and 10–4. Overall with the Yankees he was 46–24.

Al Lopez. Second place, year after year after year.

Johnny Kucks was with the Yankees from 1955 to 1959 and had one outstanding year, right down to the end. It came in 1956, when he was 18–8, and he kept right on going in the World Series, shutting out the Dodgers 10–0 in the seventh game, giving the Yankees the championship. Kucks never recaptured the luster of that fine season, dropping to 8–10 the following year. He was traded to Kansas City in 1959.

Arm trouble cut short what looked like a bright New York career for Tom Sturdivant. Joining the Yankees in 1955, Tom was 16–8 in 1956 and 16–6 the next year. He hurt his arm in the beginning of 1958 and dropped to 3–6. He was traded to Kansas City in 1959.

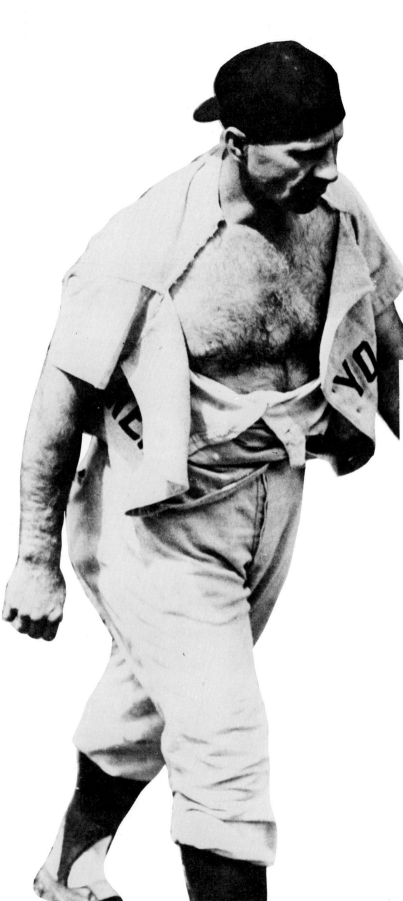

There was a brawl in Chicago between the Yankees and White Sox, and the Yankees' veteran outfielder Enos Slaughter got involved. Here he is leaving the field with his dignity intact, if not his uniform.

Enos Slaughter in more formal attire. In 1954 the Yankees acquired him from the St. Louis Cardinals, for whom he had played since 1938. He was with the Yankees in 1954 and part of 1955, when he was traded to Kansas City. The Yankees got him back from Kansas City late in 1956 and he remained in New York until midway through the 1959 season, by which time he had passed his forty-third birthday. Enos, whose trademark was nonstop hustle, batted .304 for the Yankees in 1958 as a part-timer.

Norm Siebern, outfielder. He was with the Yankees in 1956 and again in 1958 and 1959. The left-handed-hitting Siebern batted .300 in 1958, .271 the next year, and was then traded to Kansas City as part of the Roger Maris deal.

Tony Kubek's versatility made Stengel drool. Tony could play infield and outfield with equal skill. Mostly, however, he played shortstop. He joined the club in 1957 at the age of twenty and batted .297, his highest full-season mark. He played until 1965, when he was forced into premature retirement by a neck injury. Kubek is best remembered as the man who was hit in the throat by a bad-hop grounder in the seventh game of the 1960 World Series, a play which helped cost the Yankees the world championship.

Bob Turley, one of the truly hard throwers of his time. Bullet Bob joined the Yankees in 1955 and remained until 1962, by which time the last smoke had drifted from his fast ball. He was 17–13 in 1955, 8–4 in 1956, 13–6 in 1957, and then had his biggest season in 1958, when he was 21–7 and won the Cy Young Award. Thereafter he never won more than nine games in a season.

Harry ("Suitcase") Simpson was another player who made the Kansas City–New York–Kansas City circuit in the middle 1950s. The Yankees acquired him in 1957 and returned him the next year. Harry was a left-handed-hitting outfielder who failed to take advantage of the friendly right-field porch.

Pitcher Art Ditmar came over from Kansas City with Bobby Shantz and Clete Boyer in a deal which saw Tom Morgan, Billy Hunter, and Irv Noren (among others) going to K.C. Art pitched for the Yankees from 1957 to 1961, with won-lost records of 8–3, 9–8, 13–9, 15–9. Early in '61 he was sent back to Kansas City, never to win another game. The Yankees knew what they were doing in those years.

After years of glory with the New York Giants and Brooklyn Dodgers, curve baller Sal Maglie joined the Yankees in September 1957. Greeting Sal are Yogi Berra and Don Larsen. Larsen's presence was fitting, since it was against a fine game by Maglie that Don had pitched his perfect game the previous October. Sal's magic was a thing of the past, however, as he won few games for the Yankees and was dropped early in 1958.

Bobby Shantz, only 5'6", but a man who threw big, sharp-breaking curves. The league's Most Valuable Player with the Philadelphia Athletics in 1952 when he was 24–7, he came to the Yankees in 1957 in the trade that included Art Ditmar and Clete Boyer. Coming off a 2–7 year with K.C., Bobby turned it around with an 11–5 record and a league-leading 2.45 earned-run average. Used mostly in relief, he was with the Yankees through the 1960 season.

Infielder Jerry Lumpe joined the Yankees in 1956 and was with them until traded to Kansas City along with Kucks and Sturdivant for Ralph Terry and Hector Lopez in May 1959. A solid ballplayer, Lumpe was unable to crack the starting lineup despite a .340 average as a part-timer in 1957. He had some excellent years in Kansas City.

Ex-Yankee Lew Burdette after having beaten the Yankees for the third time in the 1957 World Series, giving the Milwaukee Braves the championship.

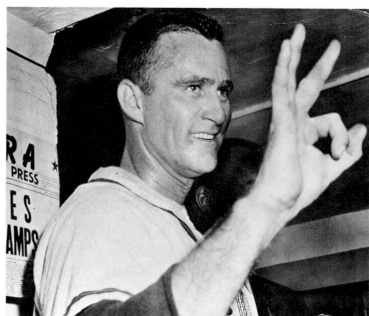

Ryne Duren, Yankee relief ace from 1958 to 1961. Duren was acquired from Kansas City in 1957 in the trade that saw Billy Martin head west. For an inning or two at a time Duren probably threw as hard as any man that ever lived, averaging better than a strikeout per inning. He was also wild and had poor eyesight, which made him even more intimidating. In 1958 his earned-run average was 2.02, the next year 1.88. He was simply overpowering during those years. Beginning to lose his effectiveness, he was traded to the Angels in 1961. After he left the game he confessed to having had a drinking problem throughout much of his career.

Yogi Berra.

Playing with the New York Mets in 1962 and 1963, Marv Throneberry became legendary for his sometimes bumbling style of play. When brought up by the Yankees in 1955, however, he had impressive minor-league credentials as a power hitter. The Yankees gave him a clear shot at first base in 1958 and 1959, but the best he could do was hit .240, which in those days meant a ticket to Kansas City. Marv went along with Bauer, Siebern, and Larsen in the big swap for Roger Maris.

Bobby Richardson, second baseman on seven Yankee pennant winners. Bobby joined the club in 1955 and became a regular in 1959, remaining so until his retirement at the age of thirty-one in 1966. Bobby was a snappy fielder and a solid contact hitter. His top years with the bat were 1959, when he batted .301, and 1962, when he batted .302, the same year he led the American League with 209 hits. A durable leadoff man, he came to bat more than 600 times for six consecutive years. His batting average for seven World Series was .305.

Right-hander Duane ("Duke") Maas came to the Yankees from Kansas City in June 1958 in a trade that saw Bob Grim and Suitcase Simpson go west. Maas stayed with the Yankees until the beginning of 1961, pitching winning ball. He was 7–3, 14–8, and 5–1 during his years as a Yankee.

Right-hander Eli Grba (that's the way he spelled it) was with the Yankees in 1959 and 1960, working mainly out of the bullpen. Eli had a moderately successful 6–4 record in '60 and then was chosen by the new California club in the expansion draft that winter.

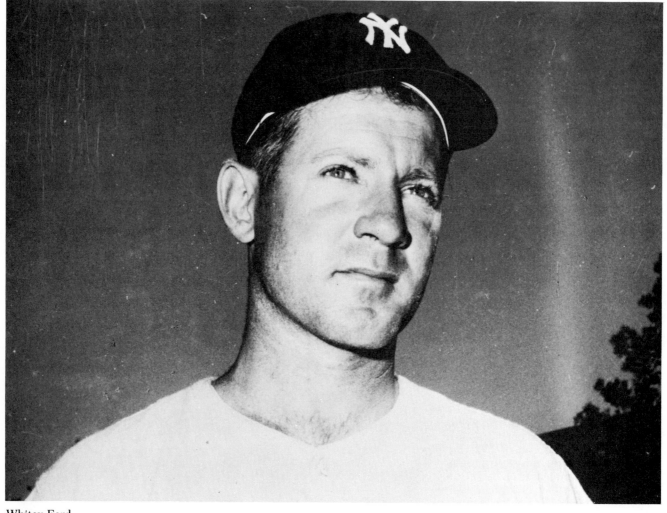

Whitey Ford.

Mickey Mantle.

An embarrassing moment for Mantle: he was fooled by pitcher Roger Craig's motion and caught off second. Shortstop Dick Groat has taken Craig's throw and is about to bring the tag down on Mickey. It occurred at Yankee Stadium in game four of the 1964 World Series with the St. Louis Cardinals.

6

From
Mount Olympus
to Down in the Valley

(1960-1969)

Roger Maris was twenty-five years old when he was traded to the Yankees. He had come to the big leagues in 1957 with Cleveland and been traded to Kansas City the next year. His batting averages were .235, .240, and .273. In 1958 he had hit 28 home runs, dividing his season between Cleveland and Kansas City.

What intrigued the Yankees about Maris was the young man's powerful left-handed stroke; it was made to order for the Stadium's friendly right-field porch. While no one could have anticipated what Roger would do in 1961, all agreed that he had a future in New York.

In addition to his batting power, Maris was also a first-rate outfielder, quick and sure, with a strong throwing arm. He was the complete ballplayer. He was also the complete small-town man. Born in Fargo, North Dakota, he was never comfortable in the big city, and particularly so when his batting feats attracted the sharks and piranhas of the press, radio, and television. He became moody, sullen, angry. Certain elements among Yankee rooters never, for some inexplicable reason, fully accepted him, despite the exciting, hustling qualities he brought to his game. Perhaps it was because he was trampling on Ruthian soil, considered sacrosanct. Perhaps it was because there was room for only one colossus in town, and Mantle had already been elected. Whatever the reason, Maris, while having one of the most fabled seasons in baseball history and exciting fans everywhere, became increasingly unhappy as it went on.

Stengel, now seventy, fielded one of his strongest teams in 1960. Only Berra and Howard among the regulars were over thirty years old. The sure-handed Clete Boyer was at third, with Skowron, Richardson, and Kubek making up the rest of the infield. Maris, Mantle, and Lopez were in the outfield.

Mantle hit 40 home runs, Maris 39, Skowron 26. Roger led the league with 112 runs batted in while hitting .283 (Maris was never a high-average hitter) and was voted MVP that year. The pitching was spotty but good enough to win 97 games and bring the club in eight ahead of Baltimore (the coming Baltimore dynasty was beginning to incubate). Ditmar led the staff with 15 wins, while Ford was held to a disappointing 12–9 season. Terry was 10–8, Turley 9–3. The bullpen was strong, with Shantz and the wild but almost unhittable Ryne Duren.

The 1960 World Series remains one of the most exciting ever played, and one of the most curious. The Yankee team batted an astounding .338 for the seven-game series and wound up losing. What the Yankees did was tear their opponents, the Pittsburgh Pirates, apart in three games by scores of 16–3, 10–0, and 12–0. Rather than being demoralized by this butchery, the Pirates of Roberto Clemente kept regrouping and coming back.

Bobby Richardson, not known for his power, hit a grand-slam homer and drove in 12 runs (he had only 26 all season). Mantle drove in 11, hitting three home runs. On the mound Whitey Ford began what became a record-breaking string of goose eggs when he shut the Pirates out twice. The only thing wrong with the whole business was that destiny entered on the side of the Pirates late in the proceedings.

The seventh game of that 1960 World Series hasn't been topped yet. Down 4–1 in the beginning of the sixth, the Yankees scored four runs and had their little lefty, Shantz, working like a machine. The Yankees beefed it up to 7–4 in the top of the eighth. Then fate took a hand. The Pirates had a man on first and none out in the last of the eighth when ex-Yankee farm hand and future Yankee manager Bill Virdon, then Pittsburgh's center fielder, hit a double-play ball to Kubek at short. The ball struck a pebble, hopped erratically and hit Kubek in the throat, gagging him. After Kubek left the game, Pittsburgh had another base hit and Jim Coates came in to pitch for New York.

Coates got two outs, but then failed to cover first base on a chopper by Clemente. Catcher Hal Smith, another former Yankee farm hand (the major leagues were decorated with these prodigals in those days), put one over the left-field wall and Pittsburgh led 9–7. Ralph Terry came in and retired the Pirates.

The Yankees still had some kick left: they scored two in the top of the ninth to tie it up. In the bottom of the ninth Ralph Terry threw two pitches to leadoff man Bill Mazeroski. Bill discovered instant immortality with the second one, sending it over the left-field wall. For the first and thus far only time, a World Series was ended by a home run.

Something else also came to an end that year. Topping and Webb had been growing increasingly impatient with their manager. Stengel, never a wholly pleasant man despite his wit and humor, had become a source of irritation to the Yankee ownership. Though the writers continued to court him as an endless source of good copy, Casey had never been overly popular with his players, whom he had always been quick to criticize, nor with a certain segment of the fans, who still considered him a foolish old man and a manager who had been given teams that couldn't lose.

At an elaborately staged press conference the Yankees announced that Stengel was retiring because of advanced age. "I was fired," the unhappy Stengel insisted. Listening to the Yankees' official line, he added, "I'll never make the mistake of being seventy again."

Stengel resurfaced two years later as manager of the newly formed New York Mets, where he suffered with teams that were as inept as his Yankee teams had been superb. He ended his managerial career where he had started it—in the second division, with a glorious interlude of 10 pennants in 12 years while running baseball's greatest team.

Another reason for Stengel's exit was that the Yankees had been priming his successor, Ralph Houk, for several years. A utility catcher for parts of eight seasons with the club, Houk had never really had a shot at the regular job because of Berra. But although the Yankees generally dealt away their nonproductive players, they kept Houk. They admired the baseball sense of this physically tough ex-Ranger major who had been awarded a Silver Star, Bronze Star, and Purple Heart in World War II. Never ones to dispose of talent no matter what form it came in, the Yankees held on to Houk as a coach and minor-league manager before promoting him to the big job. Where some of Stengel's players had come to openly ridicule and second-guess the old man, Houk won and kept the respect, admiration, and loyalty of his players. Unlike Stengel, the Major did not seek the limelight. He was a frank, forthright, extremely sound baseball man who put the feelings and welfare of his players above all else.

The American League expanded to ten teams and a 162-game schedule in 1961, the year the New York Yankees unleashed the most furious home-run bombardment in baseball history. Six players hit more than 20 four-baggers that year; one of them, reserve catcher Johnny Blanchard, was not even a regular, hitting his 21 shots in 243 at bats. Howard also hit 21; Berra, primarily an outfielder now, hit 22; Skowron hit 28; and at the top of the list was the most shattering one-two home-run punch ever, its collective total exceeding even the heyday years of Ruth and Gehrig.

It was baseball's most memorable fireworks show: Maris 61, Mantle 54. Maris, who batted only .269, drove in 142 runs in his big year (he won MVP honors again). One of Roger's great advantages was having Mantle batting behind him (Maris, despite his sizzling season, received no intentional walks that entire summer). Not only was Mantle just as hot, but it turned out to be one of Mickey's rare injury-free campaigns—he missed just nine games.

By the end of July, Maris had 40 home runs, Mantle 39. On September 1, Roger had 51 and Mickey 48. Nagging injuries were getting to Mantle now and he began missing games. Maris kept swinging. There was dual pressure on him that September; since it was the first time the schedule had been expanded, there was some question about the legitimacy of a new record's being set beyond 154 games. As it turned out, Maris ended the team's first 154 games with 59 home runs, leading the Ruthian purists to sigh with relief. He went on, however, to bang out two more in the remaining games, ending up with an incredible 61. He also ended up a nervous wreck. He never could quite understand why newsmen asked him the same questions over and over every day. Driven to distraction, he came near to a breakdown. His hair fell out in clumps, he hid from his interrogators when he could escape, gave surly answers when he could not. In short, he behaved not with the nonchalant majesty of a Ruth, but more like an ordinary human being.

Behind this cannonade, the Yankees won again, outdistancing the Tigers by eight games. Ford, whom Houk started every four days (Stengel would often hold his ace back in order to start him against certain teams and certain pitchers), had his greatest season, 25–4, accounting for almost a quarter of the team's 109 wins. Terry was 16–3. A portly reliever, Luis Arroyo, was 15–5 with 29 saves. Bill Stafford, a new man, was 14–9. Rookie Rollie Sheldon was 11–5, as was Jim Coates. It was a tough team to lose with.

The World Series against Cincinnati was a piece of cake, despite Mantle's being incapacitated after the second game with a hip injury. The Yanks took it in five. In the opener Ford tossed a shutout, and then turned in another five scoreless innings in game four. Added to his work of the previous October, Whitey had logged 32 consecutive World Series scoreless innings, erasing the old record of 29⅔ set by Ruth back in 1916 and 1918, when Babe was pitching for the Red Sox. Coming after Maris's 61 home runs it had been, as someone said later, a bad year for the Babe.

There had to be a letdown in 1962, and there was. But despite 41 fewer home runs and an injured Mantle's missing a quarter of the schedule, Houk brought his killers in five games ahead of Minnesota. Maris "slumped" to 33 home runs and Mantle to 30. Kubek went into the service but was quickly replaced at shortstop by farm product Tom Tresh, who batted .286 with 20 homers and 93 runs batted in. Richardson had a superb year, batting .302 and leading the league with 209 hits. Ford likewise "slumped" to a 17–8 season, but Terry rose to the heights with a 23–12 record. Stafford was again 14–9, and a hard-throwing rookie named Jim Bouton was 7–7.

It was like old times in the series with the Yankees playing the Giants, except that these Giants had "San Francisco" written across their uniforms. The series ran seven games and ended on a heart-stopping note. Terry took a 1–0 lead into the bottom of the ninth of game seven, when the Giants had men on second and third, two outs and their potent Willie McCovey at bat. The question was whether to pitch to the left-handed-hitting McCovey or the on-deck man, the right-handed Orlando Cepeda. Both were extremely dangerous. The Yankees elected to take on Willie, and a moment later it looked like a bad guess. McCovey pickled a Terry pitch and hit a blur—but straight at second baseman Richardson. A foot in either direction and the Giants would have been champs, and Willie McCovey would have joined Bill Mazeroski in Ralph Terry's nightmares.

Houk made it three for three as the Yankees won a fourth straight pennant in 1963, winning 104 games and finishing 10½ ahead of that familiar panting-down-the-road figure, Al Lopez. The Major did it on pitching this time; Ford surged back to a 24–7 season, while sophomore Jim Bouton was 21–7 with six shutouts. Terry was 17–15 and lefty fireballer Al Downing was 13–5 in his rookie year.

Howard, doing all the catching now (it was Berra's last year as an active player), batted .287 and was the league's MVP. The Yankees had traded Skowron to the Dodgers, but Moose was scarcely missed as smooth-gloved, power-hitting, wisecracking Joe Pepitone assumed responsibility at the bag. Joe, who was definitely not in the Yankees' laconic Italian tradition of such close-moutheds as Lazzeri, Crosetti, and DiMaggio, pounded 27 home runs in his first full year. Maris, still descending from his visit to Olympus, hit 23 home runs in an injury-aborted year. Mantle was also out much of the time with a broken bone in his foot. In 65 games Mickey batted .314 and swatted 15 home runs. With Kubek back from the service and resuming at shortstop, the switch-hitting Tresh moved to the outfield.

For the second year in a row the Yankees met transplanted playmates in the series: this time the Dodgers, with "Los Angeles" stitched across their chests. The change of climate must have been salutary, for the ex-Brooklynites handled the New Yorkers the way no Dodger team (or any other team, for that matter) had ever done in October. They cuffed the Yanks around in four straight and held them to a .171 team batting average. The Dodger pitchers, of course, were named Koufax, Drysdale, and Podres. Koufax, one of modern baseball's few supermen, fanned 15 Yankees in the opener, a new series record. Bouton and Ford pitched well for the Yankees in games three and four, but as any mathematician will attest, without scoring runs you cannot win. The Dodgers, in fact, batted only .214 to the Yanks' .171. It was one of the tamest World Series ever.

In 1964 the Yankees were challenging their own history as they went after a fifth straight pennant. They were also challenging the gods, as for the second time in four years they changed managers of a winning team. This time a promotion sent Ralph Houk upstairs to become general manager. His replacement was long-time Yankee hero Yogi Berra.

It was an interesting choice, popular with the fans, but it was not a good choice. Suddenly it was Yogi's job to tell his former teammates when to bunt, steal, take, hit away. They liked Yogi enormously, but they seemed to go out of their way to find fault with his judgment. There was probably a failing of human nature on the part of Berra's former teammates. For years Yogi had been the butt of good-natured wisecracks; now he was the manager, the supreme authority when it came to tactics and strategy. It just did not go down well.

Whether it was Yogi's fault or not, the team played sluggishly most of the year. In mid-August they were in third place behind Baltimore (managed by ex-Yank Hank Bauer) and Chicago. According to legend, it was a tune played on a harmonica that woke up the team and sent them on to a thrilling one-game finish ahead of that sturdy second-place man Al Lopez and his White Sox.

The memorable solo performance was given by utility infielder Phil Linz on the team bus after a tough loss. Berra, irritated by the loss and by things in general, asked Linz to stop playing. Linz did not. Berra became angry—probably the first and only time in his life, or at least the only time thus far recorded by historians—and began shouting at Linz, perhaps telling Phil to stuff the harmonica into a part of his anatomy that would insure its silence. Whether it was Berra's display of temper or mere coincidence, we shall never know; but from that day on the Yankees took to the field with new verve and raced to the wire, playing 22–6 ball in September and beating out the White Sox by one game.

For the second time in their history the Yankees had chalked up five in a row. Mantle batted .303, hit 35 home runs, and drove in 111. It was to be the thirty-two-year-old Mickey's last truly effective year. The accumulation of injuries was rapidly and prematurely drawing down his star. Maris, hitting the ball hard in the stretch run, batted .281 and hit 26 homers. Roger's tenure as a superstar, while memorable, was proving to have been a brief one.

Joe Pepitone put together another good year, hitting 28 homers and driving in 100 runs. Howard led the team with a .313 average, but Ellie was thirty-five and the Yankee farm system was no longer turning out catchers machine tooled for success. In addition, Kubek was suffering from injuries that in one year forced his retirement at the age of twenty-eight. The writing was on the wall.

The Yankees won the 1964 flag without a 20-game winner, Bouton's 18 and Ford's 17 being tops. Terry, his winning days over, slumped to 7–11. Downing was a bright spot with a 13–8 record, and even brighter was a young righty sinker-ball specialist named Mel Stottlemyre, who was brought up late in the season and turned in a 9–3 record.

The Yankees lost a hard-fought seven-game series to the St. Louis Cardinals, despite three home runs by Mantle and some heavy stroking by Richardson. The series's dominant figure was the Cards' fast-balling right-hander Bob Gibson, who beat the Yankees twice, fanning 31 in 27 innings.

Immediately after the series the Yankees changed winning managers once more, hiring their fourth skipper in six years. Yogi was out, reportedly for being unable to control his players or successfully communicate with them. (Yogi went right to work as a coach for Stengel's Mets.)

Even more surprising than Berra's canning was the man hired to replace him, for he was none other than the Yankees' recent conqueror, Cardinal manager Johnny Keane. Keane reportedly had been slated for the ax at season's close, but his team's surge to the pennant and world championship had saved his job. Johnny, however, had heard the rumors and resented the club's vote of no confidence, so he decided to walk out in glory. It was no doubt a highly satisfying moment for Keane. But Johnny would soon learn, to his dismay, that he was boarding an elevator that was going down, down, down.

The elevator dropped to sixth place in 1965, and then, unbelievably, to stone-cold last place in 1966, the first time since 1912 the Yankees had wound up in the cellar. By this time Keane was out and Houk had been hustled back down from the front office to take charge. But not even the Major could resurrect a fading team. In 1967 he was ninth, the next two years fifth. The four-decade domination of baseball by the New York Yankees had come to a sudden end.

There was no mystery about it. It was all very elemental—aging players and no adequate replacements. Outside of Stottlemyre, who pitched superbly during these years in the wilderness, the team had no mainstay on the mound. There would be some good work by Stan Bahnsen, Fritz Peterson, and reliever Lindy McDaniel, but it was never enough.

Ford retired during the 1967 season at the age of thirty-eight, unable to bounce back from injuries. Whitey left behind a lifetime record of 236–106, a winning percentage of .690, the best in baseball history for a pitcher appearing in an appreciable number of games.

By 1968 Mantle was playing a shaky final season—at first base—and batting .237. Richardson had retired after the 1966 season, at the age of thirty-one. Maris, bothered by injuries, hostile fans, and a shrinking batting average, was relieved to be traded to the St. Louis Cardinals after the 1966 season. Things perked up a bit for him there, including two pennants in two years, and Roger left baseball at the age of thirty-four in 1968 with a smile on his face. Tresh, who had seen his career begin so promisingly, slipped to batting averages of .233, .219, and .195 in 1966–1968. Joe Pepitone was playing center field, his early promise, too, never fulfilled. The regular catcher in 1968 was Jake Gibbs, batting .213, one point below the team average.

There were some good players, like Bobby Murcer, from Mantle's Oklahoma and supposedly Mickey's heir. Murcer did well, but he was far from another Mantle. Roy White became a good, steady, solid man in the outfield, but he was a Yankee star who might have had trouble making past Yankee teams.

In 1970 Houk raised his club to second place, winning 93 games, 15 behind Earl Weaver's mighty Baltimore club. It was a Yankee team that had an infield of Danny Cater at first base, Horace Clarke at second, Gene Michael at short, and Jerry Kenney at third. Murcer and White gave the team some pop, hitting 23 and 22 homers respectively, while a twenty-three-year-old catcher in his first full season, Thurman Munson, batted .302.

Fritz Peterson, a lefty with good control, won 20. (Fritz and another Yankee lefty, Mike Kekich, surprised fans a few years later by swapping wives; it panned out all right for Fritz and Mrs. Kekich, not so for Mike and Mrs. Peterson.) Mel Stottlemyre won 15 and Stan Bahnsen 14.

In 1971, '72, and '73, Houk brought them in fourth, watching wistfully as Baltimore and Oakland tore up the league the way the Yankees had done. In 1972 Yankee attendance dropped under a million for the first time since 1945.

By 1973 there were stirrings. For one thing, the team changed ownership once more. Topping and Webb had sold out to the Columbia Broadcasting System after the 1964 season for a reported $14 million. By 1973 CBS felt it was holding on to a bad investment and sold the club (reportedly at a $4 million loss) to a group whose chief partner was a Cleveland shipbuilder named George Steinbrenner.

"New York fans deserve a winner," Steinbrenner said at the press conference announcing the change of ownership. He went on to promise Yankee fans a winner in a few years, assuring them he would do whatever was necessary to return the team to the top. Common enough sentiments, expressed on every such occasion. Steinbrenner, however, meant it, and then some.

Ralph Houk.

Roger Maris.

Whitey Ford.

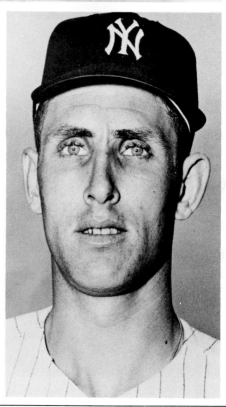

(Left)
Hector Lopez was with the Yankees from 1959 to 1966. Playing most of the time in the outfield for the club (where he had some shortcomings), Hector was a good, steady hitter. In 1959, his best year for the Yankees, he batted .283, with 22 home runs and 93 runs batted in.

(Right)
Jim Coates was a tall right-hander with an exceptionally quick fast ball. He was with the Yankees briefly in 1956, then came back for a four-year stay in 1959. Jim was a high percentage winner, with records of 6–1, 13–3, and 11–5 in 1959 to 1961. In 1962 he was traded to Washington for Steve Hamilton.

Kansas City signed Cletis Boyer to a bonus contract in 1955 and then traded him to the Yankees a few years later. Clete was with the Yanks from 1959 to 1966. The sure-handed Boyer was better known for his fielding than for his hitting, but he did hit .272 in 1962 with 18 home runs. One of the fine third basemen in Yankee history.

Luis Arroyo had bounced around in the National League for several years, without notable success. He joined the Yankees in 1960 as a relief pitcher and was 5–1. No one expected the great success he was to have the next year; Arroyo worked in 65 games for the Yankees, winning 15, losing 5, and saving 29. But just as quickly as he touched the heights, he swiftly descended. The next year he was 1–3 and soon after the 1963 season began he was gone.

October 8, 1960, and game three of the World Series has just ended. The day's hero is Bobby Richardson; he set a series record with six runs batted in.

Tony Kubek, lying on the ground, has just been struck in the throat by Bill Virdon's bad-hop grounder in the eighth inning of game seven of the 1960 World Series. Bobby Richardson has retrieved the ball and is calling for time out.

A jubilant Bill Mazeroski coming home after hitting the home run that stunned the Yankees and sent Pittsburgh into ecstasy.

Pitcher Bud Daley, obtained from Kansas City in June 1961. Bud had been a big winner with KC but never quite found the touch in New York. He was 8–9 in 1961, 7–5 the next year, and soon was gone.

Bill Skowron.

Manager Ralph Houk taking the opposing point of view. Umpire John Flaherty is trying to restrain Ralph from getting any closer to the apparent culprit, Ed Hurley. The year is 1961.

The score in 1961: Maris 61, Mantle 54.

It's a packed house at the Stadium for this 1961 game with the Minnesota Twins.

Guess whose record Maris has just tied; it came on September 26, 1961, at the Stadium against Baltimore's Jack Fisher.

The Mantle crunch.

And a few seconds later there was a new record: Roger Maris belting number 61 on October 1, 1961, against Boston's Tracy Stallard at Yankee Stadium.

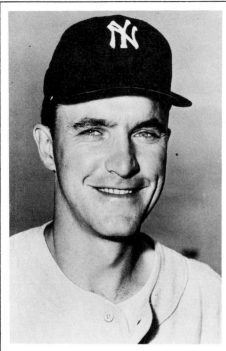

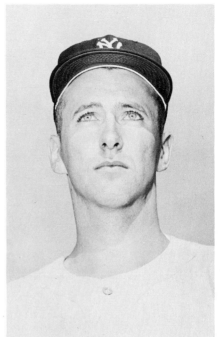

(Top left)
On many teams Johnny Blanchard would have been the number-one catcher. On the Yankees he was number three, behind Berra and Howard. Johnny was up briefly in 1955 and came back in 1959 to stay, remaining until midseason 1965, when he was traded to Kansas City. He caught, played the outfield, and pinch-hit. His best year was 1961, when he hit 21 home runs in 243 at bats and batted .305.

(Top center)
Right-hander Ralph Terry was with the Yankees from 1956 to 1964, with time out for service in Kansas City. His best years were 1961 and 1962, when he was 16–3 and 23–12.

(Top right)
Right-hander Rollie Sheldon got off to a good start with the Yankees in his rookie year, 1961, with an 11–5 record. It was his only truly effective season in New York. Early in 1965 he was traded to Kansas City.

Bill Stafford joined the Yankees in 1960. After a pair of 14–9 seasons in 1961 and 1962, arm trouble began making inroads on his career, leaving the promise of those fine early years unfulfilled. By 1966 he was pitching in Kansas City.

Joe Pepitone, with the Yankees from 1962 to 1969. Joe was a sure glove at first (where he played most of the time) as well as in the outfield. He hit with power, too, belting 31 home runs in 1966, 28 in '64, and 27 in '63 and '69. In 1964 he drove in 100 runs. His best average was .271 in '63. He was colorful, easygoing, sometimes temperamental. The Yankees were always of the opinion that Joe wasn't getting the most out of his talents. He was traded to Houston after the 1969 season for Curt Blefary.

When Tony Kubek went into the service in 1962, the Yankees replaced him at shortstop with switch-hitting Tom Tresh. All Tom did that first year was field well, bat .286, hit 20 home runs, and drive in 93 runs. When Kubek returned, Tresh went to the outfield and continued his fine play for several more years. An injury caused his batting average to begin shrinking in 1966. By 1968 all he had to show for a full year's work was a mark of .195. He was traded to Detroit the following year, his last in the big leagues.

The Yankee infield in the early 1960s, autographs and all. Left to right: Boyer, Kubek, Richardson, Pepitone.

The starting pitchers for game four of the 1962 World Series: The Yankees' Whitey Ford and Juan Marichal of the San Francisco Giants.

The Yankees did a lot of head scratching in the opening game of the 1963 World Series, as the Dodgers' Sandy Koufax fanned 15 of them for a new series record.

Mickey Mantle and Del Webb in the Yankee clubhouse.

Righty Hal Reniff appeared in 247 games for the Yankees between 1961 and 1967, all in relief. He was the bullpen ace in 1963 with 18 saves.

Lefty Al Downing threw the ball hard, leading the league with 217 strikeouts in 1964. Joining the Yankees in 1963 after brief trials in 1961 and 1962, Downing was 13–5, then 13–8 in 1964. His top win total came in 1967, when he was 14–10. He was traded to Oakland in December 1969 for Danny Cater. (Cater would later be swapped to the Red Sox for Sparky Lyle.)

Hard-throwing right-hander and future bestselling author Jim Bouton. Jim came up to the Yankees in 1962. He had his big year in '63 with a 21–7 record, following it up with 18–13 in '64, with two World Series wins over the Cardinals. Beset by arm problems soon after, he was never the same again, dropping to 4–15 in 1965. He left the Yankees after the 1968 season.

Elston Howard in 1963.

Steve Hamilton, left-hander acquired from the Washington Senators in a trade for Jim Coates early in 1963. Steve worked almost exclusively in relief for the Yankees until sent to the White Sox in September 1970. He was 7–2 in 1964 and 8–3 in 1966. Standing 6'6" and possessing a sharp-breaking curve, he was extremely rough on left-handed hitters.

Joe Pepitone.

Phil Linz, called "Supersub" because he could give you a good game just about anywhere in the infield or outfield, which is pretty much how the Yankees used him during his years with the team, 1962–1965. In 1965 he was traded to the Phillies for Ruben Amaro. Phil, also known for his harmonica playing, hit .287 in 1962, and it remained his personal high.

Mel Stottlemyre, one of the top all-time Yankee pitchers, whose misfortune it was to join the team just when its decade in the wilderness was beginning. Mel came up late in the 1964 season, winning 9 and losing 3 and helping the Yankees with the last pennant they took for twelve years. He was with the team until 1974, when a torn rotator cuff in his shoulder brought his career to an end. Had he pitched in one of the Yankees' more gaudy eras, Stottlemyre would probably have left behind a record comparable to Whitey Ford's. As it was he had won-lost marks of 20–9 in 1965, 21–12 in 1968, and 20–14 in 1969. He won 15 or more in four other seasons. His career statistics show a 164–139 won-lost record and an impressive 2.97 earned-run average. His lifetime total of 40 shutouts is second in Yankee history only to Ford's 45.

Pete Mikkelsen, a bullpen specialist, was with the Yankees in 1964 and 1965, racking up a 7–4 record in his rookie year. He was traded to Pittsburgh after the '65 season.

Horace Clarke, switch-hitting second baseman with the Yankees from 1965 to 1974. His best year was 1969, when he batted .285.

Pedro Ramos, long-time American League pitcher who was obtained by the Yankees from Cleveland late in the 1964 season. The right-hander gave the Yankees two years of superb relief pitching before being traded to the Phillies after the 1966 season. ➞

Johnny Keane.

Jake Gibbs was with the Yankees for parts of ten different seasons from 1962 to 1971. They had high hopes for the Mississippi-born catcher, looking to him to become the regular as Elston Howard began to slow down. But when he got his chance, Jake just didn't have the bat for it, hitting .233 and .213 in 1967 and 1968, the two years he did the bulk of the catching. ➞

Roy White joined the Yankees in 1965 and by the time he left the team in 1979 (he continued his career playing in Japan) he had become one of the team's fine veterans and true professionals. Four times the switch-hitting outfielder batted over .290. His best year was 1970, when he batted .296 and had career highs of 22 home runs and 94 runs batted in.

Steve Barber; the former Baltimore Orioles pitching star had lost some of his smoke by the time he joined the Yankees in 1967. The left-hander was 6–9 in half a season with the Yanks, and 6–5 the next year, after which he was let go.

Roger Maris (right), shown here with Orlando Cepeda, was traded to the St. Louis Cardinals for third baseman Charlie Smith in December 1966. Roger was delighted to get away from New York and was content in St. Louis. He played fairly well there, helping the Cardinals to pennants in each of the two years he was with them. His home-run stroke was gone, though; he hit only nine in 1967 and five in 1968.

Ruben Amaro joined the Yankees in 1966 and stayed for three years. He was the regular shortstop in '67, his .223 batting average symbolizing the team's ninth-place finish that year.

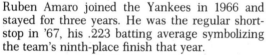

Fritz Peterson, a winning pitcher for the Yankees from 1966 to 1973. Fritz's strengths on the mound were breaking pitches, thrown with pinpoint control. He consistently worked more than 200 innings a year and seldom walked many more than 40 men. His best year was 1970, when he was 20–11. In both 1969 and 1972 he won 17 games. A wife-swapping episode with fellow Yankee left-hander Mike Kekich in the spring of 1973 made him a dubious character in Yankee eyes. Fritz had a losing record in 1973, and early in 1974 the team packaged him in a deal with Cleveland that brought the Yankees Chris Chambliss and Dick Tidrow.

Steve Bahnsen, whom the Yankees lost in one of the most unfortunate trades they ever made. The big fast baller joined them in 1966, got into a few games, and came back as a regular starter in 1968, winning 17 games. He was a steady winner for the next three years and was then traded to the White Sox after the 1971 season for infielder Rich McKinney, whom the Yankees intended to make their regular third baseman. McKinney batted .215 and was soon gone. Bahnsen won 21 games that year for the White Sox, 18 the next.

(Top left)

Bill Monbouquette, for years one of the league's better pitchers with the Boston Red Sox. The Yankees picked him up in midseaon 1967 and he was 6–5 with them. Midway along the next season, with a 5–7 record, he was traded to the San Francisco Giants for Lindy McDaniel. It was an excellent trade for the Yankees: Monbouquette had only seven more big-league appearances left in him, while McDaniel gave the Yankees six years of topnotch relief pitching and was then traded for Lou Piniella.

(Top center)

Gene Michael, with the Yankees from 1968 to 1974, and the regular shortstop during five of those years. The Yankees' future general manager and field manager batted a career high .272 in 1969.

(Top right)

The Yankees were hoping that young left-handed-hitting Steve Whitaker, who joined the club in 1966, would be able to supply some old-time power. But the best Steve could do was 11 home runs and a .243 batting average in 1967. By 1969 he was playing for Seattle.

Bobby Murcer became a regular in the Yankee outfield in 1969 after some early trials as a shortstop. A lot of people around the Yankees were predicting that Bobby would soon be replacing his fellow Oklahoman Mickey Mantle as the team's great power hitter. Bobby did not do quite that well, but he did give the team some fine years. In 1971 he batted .331, and in 1973, .304. From 1969 to 1973 his home-run totals read 26, 23, 25, 33, and 22, and his runs batted in were generally up in the low 90s. He was traded to the San Francisco Giants after the 1974 season for Bobby Bonds. In 1979 he was reacquired by the Yankees from the Chicago Cubs.

After fourteen years in the National League, Lindy McDaniel started a new career with the Yankees in 1968. Working in relief, Lindy turned in some excellent years. In 1970 he was 9–5 with 29 saves and a 2.01 earned-run average; in 1973 he was 12–6. After the '73 season he was traded to Kansas City for Lou Piniella.

Ralph Houk in the late 1960s.

While the Yankees were languishing, a sudden big noise came out of another corner of New York baseball. In 1969 the Mets, led by 25-game winner Tom Seaver, won the National League pennant and then the World Series, thus displacing the Yankees as the city's number-one team.

Some friendships are for a lifetime; others don't last quite that long. Billy Martin and Reggie Jackson early in 1977—very early.

7

Resurrection: George, Billy, and Reggie (1970-1980)

George Steinbrenner became the epitome of a new man in baseball, the owner as star. The terrain had been ploughed before, by men like Larry MacPhail, Bill Veeck, and Charlie Finley. Larry had done it with bluster and innovation, Veeck with charm and Barnum-like schemes, Finley with orneriness and a personality of flinty independence. Steinbrenner was going to do it with a relentless passion to win, backed by a bankroll that wouldn't quit. New rules were coming into baseball. Steinbrenner hadn't made them, nor did he particularly care for them, but he understood them clearly and resolved to exploit them better than anyone else. Like one of his predecessors, Jacob Ruppert, the new Yankee owner was unafraid to spend extravagantly, knowing, as Ruppert did, that no one ever lost money being successful in New York.

Steinbrenner was rich, ambitious, determined, and still had enough of the little boy in him to be intoxicated by Yankee tradition—which meant winning. For him, it also meant becoming closely involved with his new holding and fussing with it a good deal. For a major-league club owner, this is not quite the same as Mr. Macy and Mr. Gimbel doing a bit of floorwalking and nodding to the help. It was an inflammatory mix of George the fan and Steinbrenner the owner that sent him into the dugout, the clubhouse, and occasionally the team bus during spring training. Owners simply did not behave this way. But it was a new era in baseball and Steinbrenner was not only part of it, he and his checkbook were helping to shape it. When Finley, breaking up his championship Oakland club, offered left-handed Vida Blue to New York for $1 million dollars, Steinbrenner did not hesitate to reach for his checkbook, but Commissioner Bowie Kuhn stayed his hand and killed the transaction, declaring it not in baseball's best interests.

Some of his players found his presence annoying and disruptive; he saw it differently. It was his club (he gradually bought out his partners), his goodly investment, and therefore he felt it incumbent upon himself to keep an eye on it. He issued rules and regulations about tonsorial and sartorial neatness. These did not sit well with some of the free spirits who were coming into the game in the 1970s, but they adhered because they soon realized the new man meant business.

He could be generous, he could be engaging; he could also be abrupt and intemperate in his actions. Two things he never was: parsimonious and dull. He would not be outbid for a player he wanted, and he kept New York baseball at a constant boil, obtaining players, disposing of them, praising them lavishly, humiliating them cruelly, hiring and firing managers and front-office help. He may have been a problem for those closely associated with him, but for Yankee fans he was a sometimes infuriating delight as he went about resurrecting their team and restoring Yankee preeminence.

The first break in the old way of doing business came after the 1974 season when an impartial arbiter, Peter Seitz, ruled that Charles Finley had committed breach of contract with Oakland's star pitcher, right-hander Jim ("Catfish") Hunter. Hunter was thereby declared a free agent. The moment was none too opportune for Catfish, who had won 25 games that season. There he was, one of baseball's best pitchers, up for grabs. Baseball's previous salary high was in the $250,000 bracket (the White Sox's Dick Allen). The game's luminaries were about to find out what they were really worth.

After intense bidding by almost every big-league team, Hunter signed a five-year contract with the Yankees that totaled something like $3.35 million. The contract was a lawyer's delight, including not only salary but items like deferred payments, bonus and deferred bonuses, life insurance, automobiles, and lawyer's fees. Since Hunter was bound to the Yankees for just five years, his salary came to around $670,000 a year in contract time. But as far as Yankee fans were concerned, all that mattered was that they had one of the game's best on their staff. A lot of people began to realize that the Yankees' new owner was for real.

Steinbrenner, however, had not been permitted to sit in on the negotiations. The previous August he had been indicted on felony charges involving illegal corporate contributions to Richard Nixon's 1972 political campaign. Pleading guilty to lesser charges of illegal campaign contributions and a single count of aiding obstruction of an investigation, he was fined $15,000. On top of that, Commissioner Kuhn suspended him from any involvement in baseball for two years (the suspension was lifted after fifteen months).

As compelling a character as Steinbrenner was, the main action was still on the field. And it was starting to get interesting out there again. In March 1972 the Yankees had made a deal with the Red Sox and it was like old times, the Sox getting badly skinned. The New Yorkers sent shortstop Mario Guerrero and utility man Danny Cater up to Boston in exchange for left-handed relief pitcher Albert

("Sparky") Lyle. That November, after the season, the club engineered another deal that prospered for them, this time with Cleveland. The Yankees dealt off outfielders Charlie Spikes and Rusty Torres, infielder Jerry Kenney, and first baseman-catcher John Ellis for third baseman Graig Nettles and catcher Gerry Moses. The future had begun to take shape.

Houk resigned at the end of the 1973 season. The Major had never felt comfortable with Steinbrenner and it is unlikely the new owner would have retained him. Steinbrenner's first choice as manager was Dick Williams, the recently resigned skipper of the world champion Oakland Athletics, who had found he could no longer tolerate the interfering ways of his boss, Charlie Finley. Williams, however, was still under contract to Finley and Charlie would not release him from the obligation unless he received compensation from the Yankees in the form of a few young ballplayers. Finley was, in effect, offering to trade his manager for some players. He was turned down. Steinbrenner went shopping elsewhere for a manager and came up with a former Yankee farm hand and National League outfielder, Bill Virdon.

Virdon, who had had some success managing Pittsburgh, was a low-keyed man of fair-minded and honestly spoken opinions. But his lack of flair was soon to make his employer impatient, despite Bill's success in 1974. He drove his team to within two games of the eastern division title, marking the Yankees' first truly competitive season in ten years.

The Yankees' 1974 race was no fluke. With the farm system no longer as productive as in years past, the team was dealing wisely and shrewdly, thanks in part to the know-how of club president Gabe Paul, hired by Steinbrenner to run the club. In December '73 the Yankees had obtained outfielder Lou Piniella from Kansas City for Lindy McDaniel, who was about through. Piniella, a good hitter, was just getting warmed up. In April '74, just after the season had opened, Paul made another key swap. To the Cleveland Indians he sent pitchers Fritz Peterson (his winning days over), Fred Beene, Tom Buskey, and Steve Kline for first baseman Chris Chambliss and two pitchers, Cecil Upshaw and Dick Tidrow. It was one of the best trades the Yankees ever made. After the season Paul swung another one—Bobby Murcer to the San Francisco Giants for power-hitting outfielder Bobby Bonds.

In 1975 the Yankees still weren't quite ready, though the nucleus was there. Munson was an established star behind the plate, Chambliss was at first, Nettles at third, and the outfield had Bonds,

Piniella, the veteran Roy White, and Elliott Maddox, a good center fielder whose Yankee career was aborted by a knee injury.

Outside of Hunter's 23 wins in his first year in New York, the front-line pitching was not up to championship caliber. Farm product George ("Doc") Medich and two men acquired in trades, Pat Dobson and Rudy May, were adequate but no more. Lyle continued to be strong in the bullpen.

With the club playing .500 ball midway through the 1975 season, Steinbrenner tired of his gentleman manager Virdon. George had an itch to hire the recently deposed manager of the Texas Rangers, the volatile ex-Yankee Billy Martin, who was also the deposed manager of the Minnesota Twins and Detroit Tigers. Steinbrenner, as ever with his finger on the pulse of New York, sensed that Billy was not only the man for him and for the team, but for the city.

Steinbrenner sent Gabe Paul off to the trout streams of Colorado, where the unemployed Martin was trying his luck. There the agreement was reached, and a day or so later Martin took over the club at Shea Stadium, where the Yankees were tenants for two years while the Stadium was being renovated. It was, appropriately, Old-Timers Day.

It was obvious from the beginning that the Steinbrenner-Martin combine was a highly combustible one. The tough, opinionated Martin had proven in previous managerial stints that he would stand for interference from no one. Steinbrenner had already proven that he would interfere with everyone. New York baseball was in for several years of fascinating storms, thunderstorms, and cloudbursts of raging and raving.

Billy's first full season brought Steinbrenner the success he had been craving and for which Yankee fans had been turning gray waiting. The club's first flag in twelve years was won with old-time Yankee authority, on a dramatic ninth-inning home run by Chris Chambliss in the deciding game of the championship series with Kansas City.

But before the club could come all the way back, a few more pieces had to be added. Making moves like a chess grandmaster, Paul had begun soon after the end of the '75 season. He picked up outfielder Oscar Gamble from Cleveland in exchange for pitcher Pat Dobson. A few weeks later he shipped Bonds to the California Angels for a couple of moody but sterling customers, right-handed pitcher Ed Figueroa and a speed-demon center fielder who became the catalyst of the team's attack, Mickey Rivers. The same day he engineered a deal with the Pirates whereby he sent Pittsburgh Doc Medich in exchange for pitchers Dock Ellis and Ken Brett and second baseman Willie Randolph, a minor leaguer with a "can't miss" tag on him.

On June 15, 1976, Paul swung a multiplayer swap with Baltimore, sending pitchers Rudy May, Scott MacGregor, Tippy Martinez, Dave Pagan, and catcher Rick Dempsey in exchange for pitchers Ken Holtzman, Doyle Alexander, Grant Jackson, catcher Elrod Hendricks, and a minor leaguer. This trade paid short dividends for the club—Alexander and Jackson had strong seasons for the Yankees in 1976—but in the long run hurt, as MacGregor, Martinez, and Dempsey all became heavy contributors to Baltimore's future success.

Hunter, Figueroa, and Ellis each won 17 in the Yankees' drive to the pennant. Rivers batted .312, Nettles led the league in home runs with 32, Randolph had a fine rookie year, Munson batted .302 and drove in more than 100 runs, Chambliss hit the big one against K.C. and the Yankees suited up for the World Series against one of the great teams of modern times, the 1976 Cincinnati Reds. Thirty-seven years before, an earlier Yankee team had swept an earlier Cincinnati team off the field in four games. This time the compliment was returned. Led by the red-hot bat of Johnny Bench, the Reds took the Yanks easily in the minimum. Bench batted .533, edging his rival Munson, who hit .529.

That winter the Yankees moved into baseball's first free-agent market in a big way. First, for more than $2 million, they signed one of their recent conquerors, Cincinnati's hard-throwing, injury-prone left-hander, Don Gullett. A week or so later they landed free agent Reggie Jackson for a contract estimated to guarantee the slugger somewhere between $2.5 and $3 million for five years.

The thirty-one-year-old Jackson had been the big power man on the unbeatable Oakland championship teams earlier in the decade. Oakland had traded him to Baltimore, where Jackson played out his option and then sat back and allowed himself to be courted by the free spenders who were interested. Baseball fans awaited Reggie's decision with deep curiosity, although it is quite probable that he had from the beginning made up his mind to play in New York. He had already passed a covetous gaze over the big city and said, either wistfully or challengingly, that if he ever played in New York they would name a candy bar after him. The remark, which received wide circulation, seemed innocuous enough until one remembered the candy bar called Baby Ruth. It was Jackson's oblique way of letting the world know how good he thought he was.

The intelligent, articulate Jackson was always an effective self-promoter. His strong personality had been somewhat lost in the shuffle in Oakland among a team of strong personalities united in collective dislike of their less-than-congenial employer. But Jackson knew that nothing of interest was ever lost or overlooked in the media capital of the world, with its insatiable maw for goings-on. And bringing together three such man-sized and entertaining egos—Steinbrenner's, Martin's, and Jackson's—virtually guaranteed New York an interesting summer.

Actually, the first person on the Yankees Jackson upset was the team's catcher and leader, Thurman Munson. In a magazine article that appeared early in the season, Jackson was quoted as having described himself as "the straw that stirs the drink." He went on to say that Munson thought he was the straw that stirred the Yankee drink, but that Thurman could only "stir it bad." The quote was not only tactless and unnecessary, it made little sense. Munson's leadership qualities came to him quite naturally. He never sought to lead; others followed because it seemed right. He was a hard-nosed, durable, non-stop hustler, the team's veteran and premier player. He was also known to be sensitive and rather testy at times. It is unlikely that the breach with Munson opened by Reggie's straw ever healed.

It would never have been possible for Jackson to endear himself to his manager, given their respective personalities and differing viewpoints of the world at large. To Martin a Yankee superstar meant the silent DiMaggio, the stoic Mantle. It also annoyed Martin that Steinbrenner had insisted on signing Reggie (it wasn't Billy's idea) and had personally courted him. There was a bond between George and Reggie that did not include Billy. Martin's dislike of Jackson—some have called it a hatred—became an unnerving force within the already short-fused Yankee manager.

After months of sniping between George and Billy and Billy and Reggie, the Yankees staged a main event for a national television audience at Fenway Park in June. Martin accused Jackson of loafing on a ball that had been hit into Reggie's right-field sector. In a similar situation with another player, the manager would probably have waited until the end of the inning before saying or doing anything. But for Martin the time was right now; he removed Jackson from the game. Reggie, puzzled and angry, ran into the dugout, and a confrontation that was about to explode into violence ended when coach Elston Howard stepped between them.

Steinbrenner, who had witnessed the scene on television, decided then and there to fire Martin. But Billy survived, thanks in part to Jackson's intervention. Jackson's plea on behalf of his manager was probably laced with more self-interest than magnanimity—Reggie knew that being the villain in the firing of a popular manager would make his life in New York extremely uncomfortable.

The main business, however, was still on the field. While all the fuss was going on, the team was driving toward a second straight eastern division title and then another beating of Kansas City in the championship series. This time it took some real last-minute heroics—a three-run rally in the ninth inning of the decisive game to pull out a 5–3 win.

The team had been strengthened by a pair of April deals, the acquisitions of shortstop Bucky Dent from the White Sox (for a reported $400,000 and Oscar Gamble) and right-hander Mike Torrez from Oakland (for Dock Ellis). Mike gave the Yankees a solid year before opting for free agency, signing with the Red Sox.

A new Yankee ace had emerged during the 1977 season, a slimly built left-hander named Ron Guidry, who threw hard and possessed a wicked slider. Guidry had been ticketed for many things in the spring—the minor leagues, a trade (Paul talked Steinbrenner out of that one), the bullpen. Finally he became a starter and finished with a 16–7 record and the league lead in earned-run average. Figueroa's 16 wins matched Guidry for the team lead. Gullett, the club's first free agent, saw his season shortened by injuries and ended with a 14–4 record. Injuries made this talented young pitcher less and less effective, and the Yankees released him after the 1980 season. Gullett won only four games in 1978 and did not pitch at all in 1979–1980. He won only 18 games as a Yankee, meaning that the club paid him a little over $100,000 for each game he won. Hunter, too, was suffering, from a bad shoulder and a recently diagnosed case of diabetes. Catfish ended with a disappointing 9–9 record. Lyle was immense coming out of the bullpen, winning 13 and saving 26.

The 1977 World Series against the Los Angeles Dodgers was made memorable by the one-man barrage detonated in game six by Jackson. With the Yankees ahead three games to two, Jackson helped make them world champions for the first time since 1962 by blasting three consecutive home runs and driving in five runs in an 8–4 pasting of the Dodgers. For Jackson (who hit a record five home runs in the series) and the Yankees it was a dramatically tri-umphant end to a long and emotionally exhausting season.

A few weeks after the World Series, Steinbrenner went into the free-agent market burning to get one man—fast-balling relief pitcher Rich ("Goose") Gossage. Although Lyle was still one of the game's dominant bullpen artists, Gossage was even better. A burly right-hander who could throw a ball close to 100 miles an hour, Gossage was just the man to pick up a close game in the late innings.

The 1978 season made '77 look like a summer of sweet serenity. For controversy, drama, and excitement, it had no parallel in Yankee history, nor in any team's history. Ron Guidry exploded to one of the finest sustained pitching performances in modern baseball, posting a 25–3 record. Led by Guidry, who was followed by Figueroa's 20 wins, a remarkable late-season surge by the ailing Hunter, year-long bullpen heroics by Lyle and, especially, Gossage, the Yankees put on a second-half drive and overtook a powerful Red Sox club that seemed at one time to have built an insurmountable lead.

Along the way they lost their manager. There had been rumors all summer of Billy's imminent departure, despite Steinbrenner's constant reassurances. It looked at times like the owner was toying with his manager. There was nonstop sniping back and forth in the newspapers, hurried conferences between Steinbrenner and his new club president, Al Rosen (Gabe Paul had accepted a job with Cleveland), and between Rosen and Martin.

Jackson, of course, was part of the problem. Reggie's second memorable confrontation with his manager occurred at the Stadium in July. The team's star slugger, who prided himself on being a complete player, was being used a good deal as a designated hitter, a form of employment he felt cast aspersions on his talents as a right fielder. Jackson was brooding.

The Yankees were playing Kansas City the night of July 17, 1978. The score was tied in the last half of the tenth inning when Jackson came to the plate with a man on first and none out. The pitcher was left-hander Al Hrabosky. Jackson received the bunt sign. He did not appreciate it; power hitters of Jackson's stature seldom do. The pitch was a ball. Martin then took the sign off. Jackson, however, standing there in a smoldering, angry depression that had beeen building for more than a year, began bunting at one pitch after another, even after third-base coach Dick Howser made a trip down the line to tell him the bunt was off. With two strikes, Jackson bunted again, fouled it off and was struck out. Then he walked back to the dugout, removed his glasses and waited for a frontal assault from his manager.

Martin, livid with rage, ignored his recalcitrant star. Later, after consulting with Steinbrenner and Rosen, Jackson was suspended for five days.

When Reggie returned from exile, Martin was still fuming. Jackson's very presence seemed to upset and unnerve the high-strung manager. That night Billy let loose to a newspaperman a few intemperate remarks about Reggie, expanded them to include Steinbrenner, and was on his way to the block. The crusher was this: "He's a born liar" (referring to Jackson). "The two of them" (Jackson and Steinbrenner) "deserve each other. One's a born liar, the other's convicted." It was a totally self-destructive remark, as Martin must have known, and perhaps gives some insight into his burned-out frame of mind.

Martin resigned the next day in the lobby of a Kansas City hotel. He was replaced by Bob Lemon, a Hall of Fame pitcher who had once starred on the mound for Cleveland back in the days when Al Lopez was regularly bringing the Indians into second place. A man's man, Lemon was quiet and unassuming, with neither tension nor provocation in his makeup. Capable of handling any situation, his easygoing personality was usually able to defuse trouble before the sparks reached the powder keg. Released as White Sox manager just a few weeks before, he had been advised by Rosen (his old Cleveland teammate) to hang loose in the event something happened in New York.

Something did happen, but five days later it unhappened. The Yankees stunned and delighted an Old-Timers Day packed house by announcing that two years hence Martin would return as manager and Lemon would become general manager. Steinbrenner, in spite of all that had taken place, still nursed a nagging admiration for Martin's abilities and for the excitement that Billy could stir up. Billy's departure had caused howls of displeasure from Yankee fans; the volume of those howls was probably a factor in Steinbrenner's change of heart. Steinbrenner, who had produced a few shows on Broadway, never staged a more dramatic or successful production than he did on Old-Timers Day 1978.

But the business was still baseball, and the Yankees, under Lemon's quiet, steady leadership, went at it with a ferocity unmatched by any pinstripe-clad team in years. They won 48 of their final 68 games, came from 14 games behind Boston to tie the Red Sox at season's end, necessitating a one-game play-off at Fenway Park. On their most

recent visit to Fenway, early in September, the Yankees had shocked the Sox with a four-game sweep by scores of 15–3, 13–2, 7–0, and 7–4.

Behind the combined pitching of Guidry and Gossage, and powered by Bucky Dent's three-run homer, they edged Boston 5–4. Dent was the hero, but run number five, the winning run, had come on Jackson's solo shot in the eighth.

For the third straight year the Yankees played and defeated the Kansas City Royals in the American League championship series. Jackson, beaming (and performing) under the nickname "Mr. October," batted .462 in the four-game series, with two homers and six runs batted in.

It was a come-from-behind year all the way for the Yankees. After losing the first two games of the World Series to the Los Angeles Dodgers, the Yankees got into gear and took four straight. The series was highlighted for the Yankees by some spectacular glovework by Nettles at third base in game four. Three times Nettles dove for balls and made the impossible play, on two of those occasions with the bases loaded. The Yankees won the game behind Guidry, 5–1. It was estimated that Nettles's play had saved at least five runs.

For the second time in two years Steinbrenner plucked a free agent left-hander from the roster of his World Series rival. This time it was the Dodgers' Tommy John, the so-called bionic pitcher, a playing injury having caused his left elbow to be virtually rebuilt by doctors. Along with John came another free-agent pitcher, Luis Tiant, the colorful veteran from Boston whom the Red Sox had not seemed eager to sign.

To some veteran observers, the spring of 1979 felt like old times as the Yankees began getting in shape for a run at a fourth straight pennant. Twice before they had taken four, and twice they had taken five. Given the talent already on the team, given the new system whereby star players became available every autumn, and given George Steinbrenner's willingness to top the market in going after a player he wanted, it looked as though another Yankee dynasty were being put together.

It was, however, to be a season of disappointment and tragedy for the Yankees. On April 19, with the season only twelve games old, the Yankees were for all intents and purposes taken out of the race. Gossage and utility man Cliff Johnson, each big and strong, got into a clubhouse scuffle in which Gossage suffered a ligament sprain in his right thumb. (It had started innocently enough, with a few wisecracks about how well Johnson had done against Gossage when both were in the National

League. "He couldn't hit what he couldn't see," Gossage said. A few more words led to blows.) The relief pitcher missed virtually half the season, during which time the Yankees dropped out of the race. Compounding Gossage's loss was the fact that the team had traded Lyle to the Texas Rangers a few months before. Dick Tidrow became the number-one man in the bullpen, but after a few bad outings he was rather impulsively traded to the Chicago Cubs, a move Steinbrenner later admitted was a mistake. Ron Davis picked up some of the bullpen slack (he was, in fact, 14–2), but Gossage was irreplaceable.

With the club mired in fourth place and looking sluggish on the field, Steinbrenner decided to give his employees a shot of the best adrenalin he knew—Billy Martin. Lemon was replaced, and on June 19 Martin returned. There was some brave talk of another miracle, but this year the team at the top, Earl Weaver's Orioles, were not going to bend.

At the end of July, tired of missed airplanes, late arrivals at the ball park, and an assortment of other problems, the Yankees sold Mickey Rivers to the Texas Rangers. As part of the deal they reacquired the much-traveled Oscar Gamble.

On August 2, all of the club's woes, travails, and dissensions became petty and meaningless. On that afternoon Thurman Munson was taking advantage of a day off to practice landings and takeoffs in the twin-engine Cessna Citation jet he had purchased just a month earlier. Accompanied by a friend and a flight instructor, Munson came in for a landing at the Akron-Canton airport. The plane came down 1,000 feet short of the runway and crashed, bursting into flames. The other two men were able to escape, but Munson, paralyzed by the impact of the crash, was unable to move and died of asphyxiation.

Shocked and saddened by the loss of their teammate, leader, and friend, the Yankees went through the motions for the rest of the season and finished fourth. Despite this dismal conclusion to what had been expected to be another pennant-winning campaign, the club broke its home attendance record with a draw of more than 2.5 million.

Late in October, Martin brought his Yankee career to an abrupt close with a knockout punch. Billy and a friend had gone hunting in South Dakota. Upon their return they were sitting in the bar of the L'Hotel de France in Bloomington, Minnesota, a Minneapolis suburb. Martin became engaged in conversation with a man at the bar. Some words were exchanged and Martin and the man walked out of the place together, apparently to "settle" the dispute. What exactly happened in the next few minutes is subject to conflicting stories, but there was no question that the man, a marshmallow salesman, ended up on the lobby floor with a cut lip that required fifteen stitches to close. On October 28 Steinbrenner, stating that Billy's scrapes were not good for the Yankee organization, fired his manager. The two years remaining on Martin's contract, at a reported $120,000 per year, would be made good, the Yankee owner said.

It was Martin's third departure from the ball club he loved above all others. The first had come when he was still an active player, after the famous Copacabana brawl; the second in the wake of the Jackson controversies and calling his boss a convicted liar; the third after decking a marshmallow salesman. It can never be said of Martin that he went quietly or in an orthodox manner.

Billy's successor was his former third-base coach, Dick Howser. After a respectable eight-year career as an infielder with Kansas City, Cleveland, and the Yankees, Howser became a Yankee coach. At the close of the 1978 season he resigned to take a job as coach at Florida State University. Now he was back, enticed into the top job with baseball's most prestigious team, knowing full well he was going to be working for the game's most exacting, interfering, and mercurial owner.

Counting the two Martin regimes, Steinbrenner seemed to have fallen into the pattern of giving his club emotional respites in his choice of skippers, the run-down being Virdon, Martin, Lemon, Martin, Howser. Howser was more akin temperamentally to Virdon and Lemon than he was to the volatile Martin.

A few days later, on November 1, the Yankees swung a couple of deals. From the Seattle Mariners they obtained center fielder Ruppert Jones and a minor-league player in return for pitcher Jim Beattie, outfielder Juan Beniquez, catcher Jerry Narron, and a minor leaguer. Desperate to fill the gaping hole left by Munson's death, they swapped one of the club's most dependable players, first baseman Chris Chambliss, and two lesser lights to Toronto for catcher Rick Cerone and left-hander Tom Underwood.

From the free-agent bazaar the team then signed another left-hander, former Yankee Rudy May, and first baseman Bob Watson. Thus the aggressive Steinbrenner had obtained a first-rate young receiver, a center fielder, two good left-handers, and a replacement for Chambliss; the heavy-hitting Watson had batted .337 in a half-year's work with the Red Sox.

With two aces on the mound, John and Guidry,

some excellent work from May, and the incomparable Gossage sealing victories with late-inning fire, the Yankees under Howser rang up 103 victories in 1980, enough to take the eastern division title for the fourth time in five years, occupying first place from May 21 on. They dissipated a large lead to Baltimore in August but recovered and went on to clinch the title on the next-to-the-last day of the season, powered by a three-run jolt by Jackson. For Reggie it was a most satisfying season. He batted .300 (on the nose) for the first time in his career and tied Milwaukee's Ben Ogilvie for the home-run lead with 41.

For the fourth time in five years the Yankees were matched in the American League championship series with Kansas City. This time there was a stunning reversal. The Royals, after three postseason losses to the Yankees, had been priming themselves for this encounter. It almost seemed to the Kansas City players that their manhood was at stake. They played inspired ball and, led by the steaming bat of .390 hitter George Brett, swept the Yankees three straight, unleashing jubilation in Kansas City and unappeasable anger in George Steinbrenner.

Steinbrenner began picking at Howser even before the confetti had come down in Kansas City. In the second game of the series, at K.C., Willie Randolph had been thrown out at home plate on a crucial play. Steinbrenner was quick to fault the judgment of third-base coach Mike Ferraro in sending Randolph home, pointing out that he, Steinbrenner, had questioned Ferraro's competence for the job several times during the season. Baseball people almost to a man agreed that Ferraro's judgment had been correct, but they weren't the ones signing Howser's checks.

New Yorkers were then treated to a cat-and-mouse game for the next several weeks. Whether deliberately or not, Steinbrenner had manipulated the newspapers into wondering almost daily whether Howser was to be rehired. The owner would not commit himself. There was speculation that Howser could retain his job if he submitted to certain "guidelines" suggested by his boss. When Steinbrenner spoke of hiring deposed Red Sox manager Don Zimmer to coach third base for the Yankees, Howser bravely spoke up, stating he should have a voice in who coached where on his club. But it was rapidly ceasing to be his club, and on November 21 it ceased entirely. A press conference was called; the official line was that Dick Howser had resigned to pursue what Steinbrenner described as "an unbelievable" business opportunity

in Florida. The sports writers asked Howser, glumly in attendance, if he had been fired. "I'd rather not comment," he said. George Steinbrenner said, "I didn't fire the man."

In the end it made little difference. Howser was out, despite 103 victories and a division title. His replacement was the team's recently appointed general manager, former minor-league manager, former Yankee coach, former Yankee shortstop Gene Michael. When Steinbrenner went out of his way to praise Michael's fiery spirit and aggressive, combative nature, one began to understand the true reasons behind the mild-mannered Howser's dismissal. Following his pattern in the selection of his managers, Steinbrenner, unable to rehire Billy Martin, hired someone approximating him.

A few weeks later Steinbrenner signed the most avidly pursued and highest-priced player in the free-agent pool, outfielder Dave Winfield, late of the San Diego Padres. According to press reports, Winfield's contract, with salary, bonus, fringe benefits, and cost-of-living increases, could add up to $20 million by the time its ten-year duration expired. Costly, but once again George Steinbrenner had gotten his man, as previous Yankee owners had always done. It had been the Yankee tradition since the days of Ruth. The tradition had for nearly sixty years been bringing the crowds to the big ball park in the Bronx to cheer strength on the mound and dynamite at the plate. The tradition was winning, something the New York Yankees have learned to do better than any other baseball team.

The tradition that permeates the Yankees has become with time self-perpetuating, aspired to by almost every boy who swings a bat and throws a ball. The dream is to star in the great Stadium, monumental symbol of wealth, power, and success in sports. Each spring the tradition stirs again, rustling across the grass marked so indelibly by the mighty Ruth, by Gehrig, by DiMaggio, by Mantle, by all of the shareholders of Yankee history. It rises with the summer's heat and becomes October's aura, that special time of the year, the capstone of the long baseball season when the Yankees, more often than any other team, have gone forth to reassert their dominance.

Many of those boys who once dreamed the dream now crowd the record books with their achievements, and the plaques of a special few line the walls of the Hall of Fame. And many of them return once each summer to the big ball park on Old-Timers Day to stand in the sun and be saluted one more time, Yankees again for a day, Yankees forever.

Mel Stottlemyre in 1970.

Mainstays of the Yankees bullpen in 1970 posing in center field in front of the monuments to Gehrig, Huggins, and Ruth. Left to right: Steve Hamilton, Lindy McDaniel, and Jack Aker. Aker was with the club from 1969 to 1972 and gave the Yankees many good games. He was 8–4 in 1969.

Twenty-three-year-old catcher Thurman Munson, the Yankees Rookie of the Year in 1970. He batted .302.

Steve Kline, a right-hander who pitched for the Yankees from 1970 until April 1974, when he went to Cleveland as part of the swap for Chambliss and Tidrow. Steve's best year in New York was 1972, when he was 16–9 with a 2.40 earned-run average.

The Yankees acquired former New York Mets outfielder Ron Swoboda from Montreal in June 1971. He gave them part-time service until 1973, with a .261 batting average in '71 his best effort.

Injuries and left-handed pitching kept first baseman-outfielder Ron Blomberg from Yankee stardom. With the team from 1971 to 1976, Ron had some good years, batting .322 in 1971, .329 in '73, and .311 the following year. He had problems with lefties, but it was injuries that finally brought his Yankee days to an end.

The Yankees gave the San Francisco Giants $100,000 in June 1973 for former American League strikeout king Sam McDowell. It turned out to be money poorly spent; Sam was 5–8 for them that year, 1–6 the next, and then was gone.

George ("Doc") Medich, who gave the Yankees several good seasons before going to Pittsburgh in December 1975 in a key trade that brought Willie Randolph to New York. Medich's record with the Yankees from 1973 to 1975 was 14–9, 19–15, and 16–16.

Fritz Peterson.

Left-hander Mike Kekich was with the Yankees from 1969 until the spring of 1973; in March he swapped wives with Fritz Peterson; in June the Yankees swapped him to Cleveland. Mike's best year with the Yanks was 1971, when he was 10–9.

Right-hander Pat Dobson (in a Baltimore Orioles uniform) was acquired from Atlanta in June 1973 for a clutch of minor leaguers. He was 19–15 for the Yanks in 1974, 11–14 the next year, then was traded to Cleveland for Oscar Gamble.

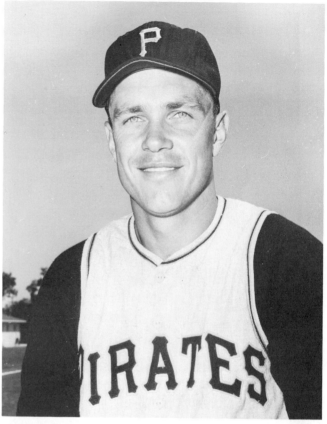

Jerry Kenney operated in the Yankees infield from 1967 to 1972, with a .262 batting average in 1971, his top year.

Bill Virdon, manager of the Pittsburgh Pirates in 1973, a year before he took over the reins of the Yankees.

Thurman Munson scoring against the White Sox on July 20, 1973, at Yankee Stadium. White Sox catcher Ed Herrmann appears unaware that the ball is lying at his feet.

Chris Chambliss.

Albert ("Sparky") Lyle.

Thurman Munson.

Bobby Bonds, obtained in a straight swap for Bobby Murcer. Bonds played one season for the Yankees, batted. 270, hit 32 home runs, then was traded to the California Angels for pitcher Ed Figueroa and outfielder Mickey Rivers.

Billy Martin. The situation looks tense.

James Augustus ("Catfish") Hunter. "He gave us respectability"—George Steinbrenner.

Fred ("Chicken") Stanley, the Yankees' regular shortstop before Bucky Dent. A handy utility infielder, Stanley was with the team from 1973 to 1980, when he was traded to Oakland.

Pitcher Doyle Alexander, obtained from Baltimore in a midseason trade in 1976. His 10–5 record that year helped the Yankees win their first pennant since 1964. He became a free agent after the season and signed with the Texas Rangers.

The colorful, controversial, and talented Dock Ellis. He came to the Yankees along with Willie Randolph in the trade for Doc Medich. He was 17–8 in 1976. The following April he was traded to Oakland for Mike Torrez.

Johnny Bench, whose .533 batting average helped grind up the Yankees in the 1976 World Series.

Willie Randolph.

Mickey Rivers.

Chris Chambliss hitting the big one against Kansas City in the bottom of the ninth inning of the fifth championship play-off game in 1976. Pandemonium followed.

The Yankees got Ken Holtzman in a swap with Baltimore in June 1976; the left-hander had had a distinguished career with the Chicago Cubs and Oakland Athletics. He was 9–7 for New York in 1976 but contributed little thereafter. He left the Yankees early in the 1978 season.

Graig Nettles.

Graig Nettles demonstrating the art of levitation.

Still not touching the ground, Nettles gets his man again.

Billy Martin explaining the other side of the story to plate umpire Bruce Froemming during the 1976 World Series.

Bucky Dent was the shortstop George Steinbrenner wanted, and Bucky was, naturally, the man George got. The deal was made in early April 1977. The White Sox got Oscar Gamble and a check reported to be for $400,000; the Yankees got Bucky.

The superb center fielder Paul Blair, long-time star of the Baltimore Orioles, joined the Yankees in 1977. The veteran Blair was employed as a reserve outfielder.

Lou Piniella, tough as flint in the clutch. He batted .330 in 1977, .314 the next year.

Roy White, the Yankees' distinguished veteran.

Thurman Munson getting Milwaukee's Sixto Lezcano at the plate.

Pitcher Ed Figueroa.

Willie Randolph and Minnesota's Rod Carew getting together at second base.

Pitcher Mike Torrez.

Don Gullett.

Pitcher Dick Tidrow.

Reginald Martinez Jackson, a young outfielder with the Oakland Athletics in 1968.

Fran Healy, reserve catcher for the Yankees in 1976 and 1977. Healy later became a member of the Yankees' broadcasting crew.

Sparky Lyle.

Bucky Dent kicking up some dirt at home plate as he is tagged out by Milwaukee's Charlie Moore.

Four Yankee starters in 1977. Left to right: Ed Figueroa, Mike Torrez, Catfish Hunter, Ron Guidry.

Billy Martin in repose.

Billy Martin in action.

Reggie Jackson sitting in front of his locker at Yankee Stadium.

Graig Nettles in 1977.

Reggie Jackson hitting his third home run in the sixth game of the 1977 World Series against the Dodgers. It was Reggie's fifth homer of the series, setting a new record. The umpire is John McSherry and the catcher is Steve Yeager, who has just looked up to follow the flight of the ball.

Bob Lemon soon after taking over the Yankees in 1978.

Ron Guidry.

Bucky Dent about to put his spikes down on home plate after hitting his memorable three-run homer against the Red Sox in Fenway Park in the pennant play-off game of 1978. Roy White and Chris Chambliss, who preceded the blow with singles, are there to greet him.

Ron Guidry.

Yogi Berra, who returned to the Yankees as a coach after being discharged as manager of the New York Mets in 1975.

Don Gullett.

Richard Michael ("Goose") Gossage.

Cliff Johnson, whose locker-room brawl with Rich Gossage incapacitated Gossage for half the 1979 season.

After trading outfielder Oscar Gamble to the White Sox in the Bucky Dent transaction of 1976, the Yankees reacquired the left-handed-hitting Oscar from the Texas Rangers in August 1979.

Bob Lemon and Ron Guidry.

Thurman Munson. Five times he batted over .300, with a high of .318 in 1975. Three consecutive years (1975–1977) he drove in 100 or more runs. His batting average for three World Series was .373.

Willie Randolph.

Filling in at second base for the injuried Willie Randolph in the 1978 World Series, Brian Doyle got seven hits and batted .438, helping boost the Yankees to the world championship.

Rich Gossage assuming a familiar role in the 1978 World Series. The departing Catfish Hunter has just flipped him the ball. Also in the picture: Thurman Munson, Billy Martin, Fred Stanley.

Tommy John beat the Yankees twice in the 1977 and 1978 World Series. The Yanks signed him as a free agent after the '78 season. If you can't beat 'em, buy 'em.

The left-handed Rudy May first came to the Yankees from the California Angels in June 1974. After a 14–12 season in 1975, he was traded the following June to Baltimore. He later played with Montreal, then became a free agent and was again signed by the Yankees in November 1979.

Action at home plate in the 1978 World Series: The Dodgers' Davey Lopes is about to be called out, the tag having been made by Thurman Munson.

Tommy John.

Rich Gossage.

Luis Tiant.

Rich Gossage.

Ron Davis.

Bobby Murcer in 1979, back for a second hitch.

Reggie Jackson.

Lou Piniella.

Reggie Jackson.

August 6, 1979, at Yankee Stadium: remembering Thurman Munson.

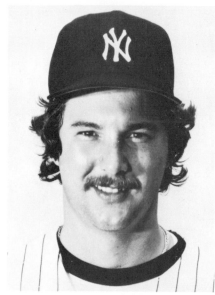

Jim Spencer, a superb defensive first baseman and a hitter with good power. Jim was obtained from the Chicago White Sox in December 1977 in exchange for a minor leaguer.

Tom Underwood.

Ruppert Jones, traded to San Diego in the spring of 1981 for Jerry Mumphrey.

Bob Watson.

Jerry Mumphrey.

Dick Howser.

Rick Cerone.

George Brett. His three-run homer off of a 100-mile-per-hour Gossage fast ball was the crusher for the Yankees in the third and final game of the 1980 championship series with Kansas City.

Dave Winfield and Gene Michael.   Dave Winfield in 1980, his last year with the San Diego Padres.

George Steinbrenner.

Epilogue

The future seems as bright and promising for the New York Yankees as their past has been glittering and surfeited. Each success extends the tradition still further; and with history as a guarantor, each success is ripe with promise of yet another.

Willing to compete with checkbook as eagerly as with bat and ball, the team is now well into what its future historians will characterize as the Steinbrenner era. Galvanized by an owner who himself seems to be as enraptured with the Yankee tradition as the most devoted fan, the team seems assured of possessing the cutting edge of success for years to come.

Free agency and quick acquisitions of star players may, for some, remove some of the game's romance. For years and years the opposition grumbled about Yankee luck in the replacement of fading stars. What else but luck could explain DiMaggio following Ruth and Mantle DiMaggio? What other team could find Berra the year Dickey retired?

But it is a new era, and for some people free agency has begun to weave a glamor of its own. And typically, as they were to exploit the home run and the farm system, the Yankees have already raised world championship flags to prove that they know how to play this new game better than anyone else.

Table of Statistics

The New York Yankees' Yearly League Standings

Year	Position	Won	Lost	Manager	Year	Position	Won	Lost	Manager
1903	Fourth	72	62	Griffith	1944	Third	83	71	McCarthy
1904	Second	92	59	Griffith	1945	Fourth	81	71	McCarthy
1905	Sixth	71	78	Griffith	1946	Third	87	67	McCarthy, Dickey, Neun
1906	Second	90	61	Griffith					
1907	Fifth	70	78	Griffith	1947	First	97	57	Harris
1908	Eighth	51	103	Griffith, Elberfeld	1948	Third	94	60	Harris
1909	Fifth	74	77	Stallings	1949	First	97	57	Stengel
1910	Second	88	63	Stallings, Chase	1950	First	98	56	Stengel
1911	Sixth	76	76	Chase	1951	First	98	56	Stengel
1912	Eighth	50	102	Wolverton	1952	First	95	59	Stengel
1913	Seventh	57	94	Chance	1953	First	99	52	Stengel
1914	Sixth	70	84	Chance, Peckinpaugh	1954	Second	103	51	Stengel
					1955	First	96	58	Stengel
1915	Fifth	69	83	Donovan	1956	First	97	57	Stengel
1916	Fourth	80	74	Donovan	1957	First	98	56	Stengel
1917	Sixth	71	82	Donovan	1958	First	92	62	Stengel
1918	Fourth	60	63	Huggins	1959	Third	79	75	Stengel
1919	Third	80	59	Huggins	1960	First	97	57	Stengel
1920	Third	95	59	Huggins	1961	First	109	53	Houk
1921	First	98	55	Huggins	1962	First	96	66	Houk
1922	First	94	60	Huggins	1963	First	104	57	Houk
1923	First	98	54	Huggins	1964	First	99	63	Berra
1924	Second	89	63	Huggins	1965	Sixth	77	85	Keane
1925	Seventh	69	85	Huggins	1966	Tenth	70	89	Keane, Houk
1926	First	91	63	Huggins	1967	Ninth	72	90	Houk
1927	First	110	44	Huggins	1968	Fifth	83	79	Houk
1928	First	101	53	Huggins	1969	Fifth	80	81	Houk
1929	Second	88	66	Huggins	1970	Second	93	69	Houk
1930	Third	86	68	Shawkey	1971	Fourth	82	80	Houk
1931	Second	94	59	McCarthy	1972	Fourth	79	76	Houk
1932	First	107	47	McCarthy	1973	Fourth	80	82	Houk
1933	Second	91	59	McCarthy	1974	Second	89	73	Virdon
1934	Second	94	60	McCarthy	1975	Third	83	77	Virdon, Martin
1935	Second	89	60	McCarthy	1976	First*	97	62	Martin
1936	First	102	51	McCarthy	1977	First*	100	62	Martin
1937	First	102	52	McCarthy	1978	First*	100	63	Martin, Lemon
1938	First	99	53	McCarthy	1979	Fourth	89	71	Lemon, Martin
1939	First	106	45	McCarthy	1980	First†	103	59	Howser
1940	Second	88	66	McCarthy					
1941	First	101	53	McCarthy					
1942	First	103	51	McCarthy					
1943	First	98	56	McCarthy					

*Won championship series. †Lost championship series.

New York Yankees' World Series Records

1921 Lost to New York Giants, five games to three.

1922 Lost to New York Giants, four games to none (one tie).

1923 Defeated New York Giants, four games to two.

1926 Lost to St. Louis Cardinals, four games to three.

1927 Defeated Pittsburgh Pirates, four games to none.

1928 Defeated St. Louis Cardinals, four games to none.

1932 Defeated Chicago Cubs, four games to none.

1936 Defeated New York Giants, four games to two.

1937 Defeated New York Giants, four games to one.

1938 Defeated Chicago Cubs, four games to none.

1939 Defeated Cincinnati Reds, four games to none.

1941 Defeated Brooklyn Dodgers, four games to one.

1942 Lost to St. Louis Cardinals, four games to one.

1943 Defeated St. Louis Cardinals, four games to one.

1947 Defeated Brooklyn Dodgers, four games to three.

1949 Defeated Brooklyn Dodgers, four games to one.

1950 Defeated Philadelphia Phillies, four games to none.

1951 Defeated New York Giants, four games to two.

1952 Defeated Brooklyn Dodgers, four games to three.

1953 Defeated Brooklyn Dodgers, four games to two.

1955 Lost to Brooklyn Dodgers, four games to three.

1956 Defeated Brooklyn Dodgers, four games to three.

1957 Lost to Milwaukee Braves, four games to three.

1958 Defeated Milwaukee Braves, four games to three.

1960 Lost to Pittsburgh Pirates, four games to three.

1961 Defeated Cincinnati Reds, four games to one.

1962 Defeated San Francisco Giants, four games to three.

1963 Lost to Los Angeles Dodgers, four games to none.

1964 Lost to St. Louis Cardinals, four games to three.

1976 Lost to Cincinnati Reds, four games to none.

1977 Defeated Los Angeles Dodgers, four games to one.

1978 Defeated Los Angeles Dodgers, four games to two.

New York Yankee League Leaders: Hitters

Home Runs

1916 Pipp 12
1917 Pipp 9
1920 Ruth 54
1921 Ruth 59
1923 Ruth 41
1924 Ruth 46
1925 Meusel 33
1926 Ruth 47
1927 Ruth 60
1928 Ruth 54
1929 Ruth 46
1930 Ruth 49
1931 Ruth, Gehrig 46
1934 Gehrig 49
1936 Gehrig 49
1937 DiMaggio 46
1944 Etten 22
1948 DiMaggio 39
1955 Mantle 37
1956 Mantle 52
1958 Mantle 42
1960 Mantle 40
1961 Maris 61
1976 Nettles 32
1980 Jackson (tied) 41

Triples

1924 Pipp 19
1926 Gehrig 20
1927 Combs 23
1928 Combs 21
1930 Combs 22
1934 Chapman 13
1936 DiMaggio, Rolfe 15
1943 Lindell (tied) 12
1944 Lindell, Stirnweiss 16
1945 Stirnweiss 22
1947 Henrich 13
1948 Henrich 14
1955 Carey, Mantle 11
1957 Bauer, McDougald 9

Doubles

1927 Gehrig 52

1928 Gehrig (tied) 47
1939 Rolfe 46

Singles

1904 Keeler 164
1905 Keeler 147
1906 Keeler 166
1927 Combs 166
1929 Combs 151
1944 Stirnweiss 146
1950 Rizzuto 150
1961 Richardson 148
1962 Richardson 158
1964 Richardson 148
1967 Clarke 140
1969 Clarke 146
1975 Munson 151

Hits

1927 Combs 231
1931 Gehrig 211
1939 Rolfe 213
1944 Stirnweiss 205
1945 Stirnweiss 195
1962 Richardson 209

Runs Batted In

1920 Ruth 137
1921 Ruth 170
1923 Ruth (tied) 130
1925 Meusel 138
1926 Ruth 155
1927 Gehrig 175
1928 Ruth, Gehrig 142
1930 Gehrig 174
1931 Gehrig 184
1934 Gehrig 165
1941 DiMaggio 125
1945 Etten 111
1948 DiMaggio 155
1956 Mantle 130
1960 Maris 112
1961 Maris 142

Runs

1920 Ruth 158
1921 Ruth 177
1923 Ruth 151
1924 Ruth 143
1926 Ruth 139
1927 Ruth 158
1928 Ruth 163
1931 Gehrig 163
1933 Gehrig 138
1935 Gehrig 125
1936 Gehrig 167
1937 DiMaggio 151
1939 Rolfe 139
1944 Stirnweiss 125
1945 Stirnweiss 107
1948 Henrich 138
1954 Mantle 129
1956 Mantle 132
1957 Mantle 121
1958 Mantle 127
1960 Mantle 119
1961 Mantle, Maris 132
1972 Murcer 102
1976 White 104

Stolen Bases

1914 Maisel 74
1931 Chapman 61
1932 Chapman 38
1933 Chapman 27
1938 Crosetti 27
1944 Stirnweiss 55
1945 Stirnweiss 33

Batting Average

1924 Ruth .378
1934 Gehrig .363
1939 DiMaggio .381
1940 DiMaggio .352
1945 Stirnweiss .309
1956 Mantle .353

New York Yankee League Leaders:
Pitchers

Wins

1904	Chesbro	41
1906	Orth	27
1921	Mays (tied)	27
1927	Hoyt	22
1928	Pipgras (tied)	24
1934	Gomez	26
1937	Gomez	21
1938	Ruffing	21
1943	Chandler (tied)	20
1955	Ford (tied)	18
1958	Turley	21
1961	Ford	25
1962	Terry	23
1963	Ford	24
1975	Hunter (tied)	23
1978	Guidry	25

Earned-Run Average

1920	Shawkey	2.45
1927	Moore	2.28
1934	Gomez	2.33
1937	Gomez	2.33
1943	Chandler	1.64
1947	Chandler	2.46
1952	Reynolds	2.07
1953	Lopat	2.43
1956	Ford	2.47
1957	Shantz	2.45
1958	Ford	2.01
1978	Guidry	1.74
1979	Guidry	2.78
1980	May	2.47

Strikeouts

1932	Ruffing	190
1933	Gomez	163
1934	Gomez	158
1937	Gomez	194
1951	Raschi	164
1952	Reynolds	160
1964	Downing	217

Most Valuable Player Awards
(Instituted in 1931)

1936	Lou Gehrig	
1939	Joe DiMaggio	
1941	Joe DiMaggio	
1942	Joe Gordon	
1943	Spud Chandler	
1947	Joe DiMaggio	
1950	Phil Rizzuto	
1951	Yogi Berra	
1954	Yogi Berra	
1955	Yogi Berra	
1956	Mickey Mantle	
1957	Mickey Mantle	
1960	Roger Maris	
1961	Roger Maris	
1962	Mickey Mantle	
1963	Elston Howard	
1976	Thurman Munson	

Rookie of the Year Awards
(Instituted in 1947)

1951	Gil McDougald
1954	Bob Grim
1957	Tony Kubek
1962	Tom Tresh
1968	Stan Bahnsen
1970	Thurman Munson

Cy Young Awards
(Instituted in 1956)

1958	Bob Turley
1961	Whitey Ford
1977	Sparky Lyle
1978	Ron Guidry

Bibliography

Anderson, Dave; Chass, Murray; Creamer, Robert; Rosenthal, Harold. *The Yankees*. New York: Random House, 1979.

Baseball Encyclopedia. New York: Macmillan, 1979.

Creamer, Robert. *Babe*. New York: Simon and Schuster, 1974.

Dickey, Glenn. *The History of American League Baseball*. New York: Stein and Day, 1979.

Golenbock, Peter. *Dynasty*. Englewood Cliffs, N.J.: Prentice-Hall, 1975.

Honig, Donald. *Baseball When the Grass Was Real*. New York: Coward, McCann, Geoghegan, 1975.

———. *Baseball Between the Lines*. New York: Coward, McCann, Geoghegan, 1976.

———. *The Man in the Dugout*. Chicago: Follett, 1977.

———. *The October Heroes*. New York: Simon and Schuster, 1979.

Lyle, Sparky; Golenbock, Peter. *The Bronx Zoo*. New York: Crown, 1979.

Mosedale, John. *The Greatest of All: The 1927 Yankees*. New York: Dial Press, 1974.

Ritter, Lawrence S. *The Glory of Their Times*. New York: Macmillan, 1966.

Ritter, Lawrence S.; Honig, Donald. *The Image of Their Greatness*. New York: Crown, 1979.

Salant, Nathan. *This Date in New York Yankee History*. New York: Stein and Day, 1979.

Smith, Robert. *Baseball*. New York: Simon and Schuster, 1970.